WHAT GOD IS DOING

What God is Doing: Old Testament Object Lessons for Kids

ISBN: 978-0-9981968-2-4 (print), 978-0-9981968-3-1 (epub)

Religious Kids Graphics by Pixel Paperie

Publishing and Design Services: MartinPublishingServices.com

WHAT GOD IS DOING

Old Testament Object Lessons for Kids

ANNE MARIE GOSNELL

DEDICATION

■ ■

This book is dedicated to my students:

Southside Christian School
(1997-2000)

Oconee Christian Academy
(2001-2003)

Central First Baptist Church
(2000-2004)

First Baptist Church Gowensville
(2007-2017)

And to any future children in my ministry.

I pray you will love Jesus and serve Him faithfully.

CONTENTS

■ ■

CONTENTS

CONTENTS

■ ■ ■ ■ ■ ■ ■ ■ ■ ■ ■ ■ ■ ■ ■ ■ ■ ■ ■ ■

INTRODUCTION

W*hat God is Doing: Old Testament Object Lessons for Kids* includes 25 interactive lessons for children ages 5 to 12. These weekly lessons are meant to last 20-30 minutes. I believe the title, *What God is Doing*, correctly depicts how God began to bring about His plan of salvation. God worked through imperfect people and used a nation as a channel to provide a way of salvation for all mankind.

This curriculum will help you:

- teach engaging Bible lessons children cannot resist.
- create a fun teaching atmosphere that sparks the imagination of children.
- teach children Biblical truth that enhances their spiritual growth.
- share the gospel with children and expand the Kingdom.

I am humbled that you have chosen to use this resource! I pray that it will ignite a passion for Jesus in those who hear you teach.

For more resources for parents and teachers, visit https://www.futureflyingsaucers.com/wgid-resource-page/.

To receive weekly Bible lessons, book updates, and children's ministry helps, subscribe at https://www.futureflyingsaucers.com/.

Keep on keeping on, my friend!

Anne Marie Gosnell

futureflyingsaucers.com

Behold, I WILL DO something new, Now it will spring forth;
Will you not be aware of it? I will even make a
roadway in the wilderness, Rivers in the desert.

—Isaiah 43:19

HOW THIS BOOK WORKS

■ ■

I have put these lessons in an order that encourages spiritual growth. However, the lessons do not have to be taught sequentially. These lessons can be taught with large groups or small groups. When planning your Bible lessons, whether at home or church, determine your objective first. Then look through the Table of Contents and decide which lessons will best help you reach your objective.

Each lesson has a **free downloadable poster** that you can access from the **Resources Page** (https://www.futureflyingsaucers.com/wgid-resource-page/). Discuss and display the posters in the room throughout this series, and read them each week. You can choose to use the shorter verses as memory verses. Other lesson freebies can be found on the **Resources Page** (https://www.futureflyingsaucers.com/wgid-resource-page/) as well.

Many lessons have a **Background** section. This summarizes the events that "set the stage" for the lesson. Use this section to help you put the lesson into context for the children.

Old Testament history takes place in a variety of locations; therefore, there is a **Geography** section for each lesson. I encourage you to have a map to point out these places. See the **Resources Page** (https://www.futureflyingsaucers.com/wgid-resource-page/) for maps.

The **Object Lesson** is usually first and might be referred to throughout the lesson. Most of the objects are items that many children know and see daily. Jesus used common objects such as sheep and trees when He taught, and we can do the same. Preparation time is minimal, and most lessons use materials you will find around your home. I do suggest practicing the lessons ahead of time to be sure you understand how the activity works.

The **Bible Lesson** section is a paraphrase of the event from the **Scripture Focus**. Read the Scripture to prepare for teaching your lesson. Afterward, read the Bible Lesson section a few times. Practice enough so that you can tell the story without reading.

The last section is essential: **Life Application**. This is where Scripture "comes alive" and the kids learn how to apply it to their lives. If we do not explain the purpose of Scripture to children, then you and I have failed as Bible teachers. All Scripture is useful, and we must showcase the glorious purpose of the Bible in each lesson.

At the end of each lesson is a **Comment Box**. This is an area for you to reflect upon your teaching so you can improve your skills. Thinking retrospectively will help you to evaluate your personal ministry. Ask yourself two questions: *"What went well as I taught this lesson?"* and *"What can I do better?"*

I would love to know how your lessons go! Feel free to contact me at futureflyingsaucers@klopex.com. You can also join my Facebook group, Bible Lessons for Kids.

A FEW LAST TIPS

■ ■

Encourage the children to use their Bibles. Do not assume they think your story is Biblical just because you tell it. Have them be like the Bereans in the book of Acts. Show them in the Bible the verses you will be using. Some of the lessons will have the kids either reading along with you or reading for themselves. If you have children who do not read, you can still help them find the reference in the Bible. This is a great habit to begin when young.

When you teach a lesson, try not to say words such as, *"Our story today comes from..."* While the Bible is the story of God, it is more than a story. We live in a world where the line between fairy tales, fiction, and truth is blurred. So, refer to every person or event as history or biography. Children need to understand that people in Scripture were **real**, breathing people. The places in the Bible were—and some still are—**real** places.

Be enthusiastic when you teach. Do not put on a show, but share the joy of Jesus so that He is contagious! Scripture tells us that if Jesus is lifted up, He will draw all men to Him. Let us lift Him up!

One last thing...NEVER be afraid to share your testimony! Someone in the room might need to hear how God has worked in your past, how He is working today, and what He is doing in your future.

1 HOW DID WE GET HERE?

■■■■■■■■■■■■■■■■■■■■■■■■

There are times when Christians are accused of not thinking logically. Christians are accused of not looking at evidence. These accusations are pointing out that Christians have a biblical worldview. Instead of looking at the world and then making decisions, Christians look to the Bible first and then make decisions about the world around them.

Scripture Focus: Genesis 1

Materials:

- Legos or blocks that can build a structure
- Letters from a word game that spell "CREATION"
- White board
- Genesis 1:3 poster

{Create a Lego creation. I had someone make a helicopter and a boat for me. Also have a bowl of loose Legos.}

Geography: The universe

Background: The Creation event is the source of much debate in our world. It is important to realize that one's view of Creation will either enhance or weaken a faith in God.

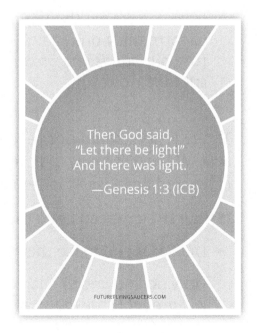

Then God said,
"Let there be light!"
And there was light.

—Genesis 1:3 (ICB)

FUTUREFLYINGSAUCERS.COM

OBJECT LESSON

■ ■

{Show the children the spelling letters. Spread them out on the table and move them around to spell the word "CREATION." Then pick up the letters.}

I am going to drop these letters, and the word "CREATION" will be spelled again.

{Drop the letters. They should be in random order.}

{Ask:}

- Did the letters spell the word "CREATION"? [*No*]

- Why not? [*Allow for answers.*]

- How can we get the letters to form the word again? [*Use our hands and brains to spell the word.*]

Those letters could not rearrange themselves to make any sense. We had to do that. We had to know the order of the letters so the word would be correct. A word is created because of letter rules and vocabulary. Chaos cannot create order.

{Show the created Lego model and ask:}

- Did someone make this? [*Yes*]

- How do you know? Did you see the person make it? [*Allow for answers. They will probably say that they know because the model could not be made by itself.*]

I want you to make one of these Lego models. I want you to create your own Legos and then make the model.

{The children will argue that they cannot do that. Show the bowl of loose Legos and ask:}

- Can you make Legos out of nothing? [*No*]

- If you speak to this pile of Legos will they create the model? [*No*]

- Try it. On the count of three, I want everyone to say, "Legos, make a model [whatever the model example is]!" Ready? [*Allow children to say the words.*]

- Why did this not work? [*Allow for answers.*]

You must use your fingers and materials, such as Legos, to create something. You must use your brain and imagination. You are a designer because you can create objects, paintings, or pictures.

God is the ultimate Creator. He is all-powerful! God created with intelligent design. Everything God created has a purpose and everything has its place.

BIBLE LESSON

We need to agree to a set of basic rules before we begin this lesson. First, we need to state that God exists (Psalm 14:1). Second, we need to state that the entire Bible is from God (2 Timothy 3:16). Last, we need to state that God is all-powerful (Matthew 19:26).

{As you list each truth, ask the children if they agree with it. Explain it if needed.}

These foundational truths are important. The Scriptures that tell us how the world was made and how people were created are remarkable. In fact, the Scriptures are so remarkable that many people say Genesis 1 and 2 are descriptive like a poem and are not factual.

Many scientists state that the Creation event cannot be correct because it does not reflect scientific fact. Let us go back to our basic rules and think logically. If God exists, and the Bible is from God, and God is all-powerful, then let us read what Genesis tells us about how the world was created. It must be true.

{Read Genesis 1:1-27. Use the ESV Bible if possible. Draw on the board what happens as God creates it.}

{Ask:}

- Does the Bible tell us in detail how God made everything? [*No*]

- Does the Bible tell us Who created the universe? [*Yes*]

- How long is one day? [*24 hours*]

- For each day, the Bible says, *"And it was morning and it was evening."* Why? [*God wants us to know that it took Him 24 hours to create on each day.*]

- Were people around when God created the universe? [*No*]

- If people were not around when God created the universe, then how do we know what happened? [*If you believe the Bible, then you know what happened. If people do not believe in the Bible, then they do not know what happened.*]

Christians are accused of not thinking about Creation in a scientific manner. What many people do not understand is that Christians read the Bible for answers first and then study science. God created science; science does not create God.

LIFE APPLICATION

■ ■

Many scientists over the years knew that there was a God and that He was the Creator. Examples include Isaac Newton (laws of motion), Johannes Kepler (laws of planetary motion), Albert Einstein (theory of relativity), Blaise Pascal (mathematician and physicist), and Werner von Braun (NASA's moon project).

{Pick up the created model.}

These scientists understood that something that is created must have a Creator. Although this Lego model might be difficult for some people to design, it cannot compare to how difficult it is to make a frog, or an eyeball, or a mountain.

The book of Romans says that all of creation tells us that there is a God. Unfortunately, many people choose to worship nature instead of the God who made it.

Make sure that you are a person who knows the Bible. Make sure you are a person who asks questions. Do not believe something just because an adult tells you it is true—even in church. Read your Bible. Figure out the answer for yourself.

Be a person who thinks.

What can we learn from Creation? Everything was created by God who is all-powerful. He is an Intelligent Designer.

COMMENT BOX

■ ■

THINK: What went well as you taught this lesson? What can you do better?

_____

_____

_____

_____

_____

_____

_____

_____

_____

_____

TIP: Do you have a true Biblical worldview? Ask God what you should believe about Creation.

2 WHY DO PEOPLE DO BAD THINGS?

Have you ever heard anyone ask, *"Why do people do bad things?"* Many say there is not an easy answer. Is that correct? Those of us with a Biblical worldview go to the Bible first when tough questions arise. How does the Bible answer this question? This Adam and Eve object lesson will help.

Scripture Focus: Genesis 2-3

Materials:

- Candle
- 3 small balloons filled with air
- 1 balloon filled with water
- Wet washcloth
- Candle lighter
- Fire extinguisher (just in case!)
- Genesis 3:15 poster

I will make you and the woman enemies to each other. Your descendants and her descendants will be enemies. Her child will crush your head. And you will bite his heel.

—Genesis 3:15 (ICB)

Geography: No one knows the exact location of the Garden of Eden, but we do know the location of the Tigris and Euphrates Rivers.

Background: Genesis 1 talks about Creation and tells us that God made everything. On days one through three, He created the scenery: light, darkness, oceans, atmosphere, and land with vegetation. During days four through six, He created the objects that filled the scenery: sun, moon, and stars; ocean animals; birds; and land animals. He also created man on the sixth day. God looked at everything He had made and thought it was good. But when He looked at man, He didn't say, *"It is good."* Instead God said, *"It is VERY good."*

BIBLE LESSON

{Put the unlit candle in front of you. Have the balloons beside you out of the way.}

In Genesis 2, we are told how God made man. We learn in Genesis 1 that God created all of the other items by speaking. But when He made man, God formed him from the dust of the ground. God then breathed His own breath into the body, and humanity was created. He did not do that with animals.

Right from the start, people were different from animals and the other things God created. In fact, God put people in charge of the animals and the garden.

{Ask:}

- Does this mean we can treat animals poorly and devastate the land? [*No*]

- How would God want us to treat animals? [*Allow answers. Include the answer of treating animals with kindness.*]

- How would God want us to treat the environment? [*Allow answers. Help the kids to know we need to be good stewards and use the land responsibly.*]

Adam walked with God in the garden. They had a perfect relationship. Adam named all the animals, but he could not find a suitable helper. The Lord caused Adam to fall into a deep sleep and removed one of his ribs. God formed Eve from the rib and presented her to Adam. They lived in the garden and all was peaceful. But there was one tree from which God said they were not to eat: The Tree of the Knowledge of Good and Evil.

There was a serpent who was crafty, deceitful, and cunning. The serpent found Eve in the garden.

{Light the candle.}

He began to ask her questions and put doubts in her mind about who God was and what He said. The serpent asked Eve about the fruit on the tree. Eve considered the fruit and thought: *It was beautiful. It was good for eating.*

{Point to the candle.}

This candle is beautiful! The flame shines and flickers so nicely. Eve saw that the fruit was beautiful. She picked the fruit and ate it. She gave some to Adam. He ate it, too.

{Ask:}

• What sins did Adam and Eve commit? **{Allow for answers: disobedience, arrogance, selfishness, pride. As the kids list them, pick up each air-filled balloon and pop it over the candle. Each time the balloon bursts, the candle will blow out. Relight the candle. After the last one, show the broken balloon pieces.}**

God then came to see Adam and Eve. Adam and Eve hid because they were ashamed. They recognized that they were naked.

{Hold up the rubber of the broken balloons.}

Their relationship with God was broken. Could Adam and Eve do anything to fix their broken relationship? No. In fact, God had to punish them. They did wrong. They had to leave the perfect garden.

Because of the sins of Adam and Eve, pain and disease entered the world. Women now have great pain when they have babies. Weeds and thistles appeared, and it was much harder for Adam to garden and work the land. Men now work hard to provide for their families.

The serpent was cursed as well. God placed hatred between the snake and the children of the woman. In fact, one day that serpent would bite the heel of one of her children, but then that Child would turn around and crush the head of the serpent.

{Ask:}

• Who is the Child that will crush the serpent's head? [*Jesus*]

Adam and Eve had babies. Their babies grew up and had babies. Every baby that was born had a broken relationship with God. And this is how you and I are. We are born into sin. There is no way we can have a perfect relationship with God because of our sin. This is what it means in the Bible when it says, *"All have sinned."*

{Ask:}

• Can you put the balloons back together? [*No*]

LIFE APPLICATION

■ ■ ■ ■ ■ ■ ■ ■ ■ ■ ■ ■ ■ ■ ■ ■ ■ ■ ■ ■

We cannot fix our broken relationship, and God knows that. Immediately after the events in Genesis 2 happened, God began working on His plan to bring people back to Him.

{Show the water balloon.}

The purpose of the Old Testament is to teach us what God does to fix our sin problem. The New Testament tells us Who fixes the sin problem: Jesus.

{Ask:}

- What does John 3:16 tell us that God did? [*Have the children quote the verse, if possible. If not, say or read the verse to them. God gave us Jesus, His Son.*]

- What do we have to do to have eternal life? [*We must believe in Jesus.*]

- What does eternal life mean? [*Allow answers. Explain that eternal life means that the relationship with God is no longer broken. We will be with God and Jesus forever.*]

God loved the world so much that He sent Jesus. If we believe in Jesus, we will have everlasting life.

{Hold the balloon over the candle. It will not pop.}

John 7:38 tells us that whoever believes in Jesus has living streams of water that will flow from within him. Jesus lives in us, just like the water in this balloon.

{Ask:}

- If we believe in Jesus, does that mean we never sin? [*No*]

{Show the bottom of the balloon. The balloon should be blackened from the candle.}

Christians do sin, and it blackens us. Sin does not break our relationship with Jesus, but it does harm our relationship with Him. Sin also messes up our relationships with other people. But when Christians sin, we can ask for forgiveness.

{Wipe the black away with the wet washcloth. Most of the black should come off.}

Jesus is the One who makes us righteous. He is the One who cleanses us from all unrighteousness. We cannot do it.

What can we learn from Adam and Eve? We must understand that sin entered the world because of people, and that God fixes the sin problem through Jesus Christ.

COMMENT BOX

■ ■

THINK: What went well as you taught this lesson? What can you do better?

_____

_____

_____

_____

_____

_____

_____

_____

_____

TIP: This book is called *What God is Doing* because the Old Testament is setting the stage for salvation. God is at work all throughout history.

3 CAIN AND ABEL

■ ■

Sin is a big deal. People don't like to admit that, but it is true. If it was not really a big deal, then why did Jesus give up His life to save us from sin? Even during the beginning of civilization, blood sacrifice represented forgiveness and redemption. Knowing the difference between the offerings of Cain and Abel helps us to understand Jesus a little better.

Scripture Focus: Genesis 4:1-15

Materials:

- Cookie sheet or shallow pan
- Red food coloring
- Vinegar (Add a few drops of red food coloring and stir.)
- Small cup (I used an applesauce cup. Use a permanent marker to draw an angry face on the cup.)
- Baking soda (Put 2-3 tsp. in cup.)
- Lego people
- Genesis 4:7 poster

"If you do good, I will accept you. But if you do not do good, sin is ready to attack you. Sin wants you. But you must rule over it."

—Genesis 4:7 (ICB)

FUTUREFLYINGSAUCERS.COM

Background: Adam and Eve had eaten of the forbidden fruit, and they were no longer welcome in the garden. Sin caused a broken relationship with God. Because of the sins of Adam and Eve, women now have great pain when they have babies. There is disease and heartache. Men must work hard to provide for their families. God placed hatred between the serpent and the children of the woman. But one day that serpent will bite the heel of one of her children, and then that Child will turn around and crush the head of the serpent.

BIBLE AND OBJECT LESSON

■ ■

{Put the cookie sheet on a table in front of you. Have the other items to the side.}

Eve gave birth to Cain and then Abel. Her children did wrong just like you and I do wrong. No one taught you to do wrong things. Adam and Eve had to discipline their children just like your parents discipline you. This is because all people sin. Every person is born with a nature to sin.

As the boys grew up, Cain became a farmer and Abel became a shepherd. One day, both brought offerings to God. Cain brought the first fruits of his crops. Abel brought a spotless lamb. To us, both offerings seem to be acceptable. Both offerings reflect the jobs of those who were giving. However, Abel's offering was accepted. Cain's offering was not.

Cain became very angry and his countenance fell.

{Show the angry cup to the children. Put it in the middle of the cookie sheet.}

His emotions became violent and filled with hatred. Even though Cain had not done anything physically wrong, God could see his heart. Jeremiah 17:9 says, *"The heart is deceitful above all things, and desperately wicked."* The word "deceitful" means "misleading." The word "desperately" means "extremely." That verse in Jeremiah tells us that our hearts will mislead us and that they are extremely wicked. When we are born, we are born sinful. We have a sin problem, and so did Cain.

{Ask:}

- Why do you think Cain's sacrifice was not accepted and Abel's was? [*Allow for answers. Lead the children to think about other sacrifices from the Bible: those in the Temple, Abraham and Isaac, the blood over the doors of Passover, etc. However, in Leviticus, God requires grain offerings and first fruits of the harvest. Scripture is not totally clear why Cain's sacrifice was not accepted by God, but we do know that God is always right.*]

God went to Cain and asked, *"Why are you angry? Do what is right. Sin is waiting for you!"*

Cain did not listen to God. Instead, Cain went to talk to Abel, and he killed Abel in a field.

God went to Cain again and asked, *"Where is your brother?"*

Cain responded angrily, "Am I supposed to take care of my brother?"

God replied, *"What have you done? I hear your brother's blood calling from the field."*

{Ask:}

- Did God already know why Cain was angry? [*Yes*]
- Did God know where Abel was? [*Yes*]
- Why do you think God asked Cain those questions when He already knew the answers? [*Allow for answers. Lead children to think about why teachers ask questions. They want their students to think.*]

God wanted Cain to think about what he had done. Conviction, or realizing you have done wrong, can be a hard lesson to learn. Because we sin, we are guilty. We are convicted of doing wrong.

{Ask:}

- When a defendant is told by a judge that he did wrong, what is that called? [*Being convicted of a crime*]
- What usually happens to a convicted prisoner? [*He must go to prison. He must pay a penalty.*]
- When we sin who do we sin against? [*God*]
- Who do we hurt when we sin? [*Ourselves and others*]

Cain allowed the sin to grow in his heart. The anger and jealousy that he felt not only affected Cain's behavior, but also hurt his brother, Abel. **When we choose to sin, it bubbles out of us and can hurt those around us.** Cain killed his brother. Sin can destroy not only those who sin, but also those around the sinner.

{Put Lego people around the cup. Add the vinegar to the mix of baking soda in the cup. Watch as the sin takes out the Lego guys.}

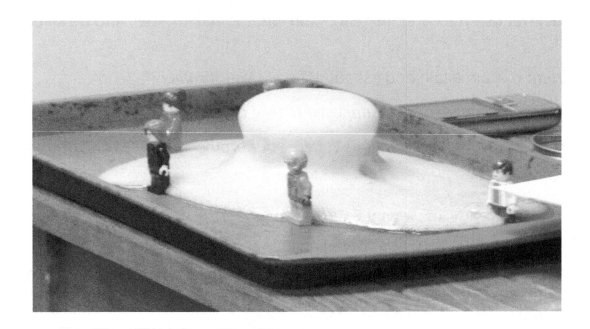

{Ask:}

- When you see red, what emotion do you think of? [*Anger*]
- Who was hurt by Cain's sin? [*Abel, Adam, Eve, and Cain*]
- Can you think of an example of a sin you did that hurt you and maybe another person? [*Allow for answers.*]

LIFE APPLICATION

■■■■■■■■■■■■■■■■■■■■■■■

We need to pay attention to our hearts. We need to think about the people around us. **God gives us second chances to change our behavior and do what is right.** Scripture tells us that when we are tempted to do wrong, there will always be a way out. God gave Cain a chance to do better. But Cain became angry and the sin was his anger.

Many times, even before we do something wrong, God will talk to your hearts with a small voice and warn you to not do that wrong thing. Sometimes that voice tries to stop your thoughts. You need to listen to it.

If you do choose to sin, God will use the Holy Spirit to convict you of your sin. You get an awful feeling inside when the Holy Spirit convicts you. That is called "feeling guilty."

When you sin, you must pay a penalty. Cain's penalty was to be a wanderer and a fugitive for the rest of his life. God said that the ground would never produce for him again. He would never stay in one place to live. Because of your sin, you deserve a penalty.

We are not alone in our sin. That Lego guy got wiped out by the other person's sin! **We are not in our sin alone.** Decisions we make affect other people. We need a solution to this sin problem! Sin may look like fun at the start, but in the end, sin is no fun. No one is truly happy in sin. It is wonderful to know that God gives us second chances to do the right thing!

Our sin means we have a penalty. Scripture says that the penalty for sin is death. Something or someone has to die. God sent Jesus to earth. Jesus, who was perfect and not guilty, took our penalty instead. He died on the cross and blood was shed.

What can we learn from Cain and Abel? Sacrifice must be offered by faith. Life is in the blood. The penalty for sin is death. Jesus took our penalty and it is His blood that sets us free from sin.

COMMENT BOX

■ ■

THINK: What went well as you taught this lesson? What can you do better?

_____

_____

_____

_____

_____

_____

_____

_____

_____

TIP: It is important to teach the concept of sacrifice. If we can help kids see the reason Jesus had to die, it helps them to better understand the idea of being a living sacrifice.

NOAH AND THE FLOOD

The story of Noah is not a beautiful poster of a man with cute animals. The Flood was the response from God after the people had grossly sinned. This Noah and the Flood object lesson will help our kids describe why God flooded the earth, how God saved humanity, and why God always chooses a remnant.

Scripture Focus: Genesis 6-9

Materials:

- 2 cups of water in a closed zipper sandwich bag
- 9 child volunteers (If you do not have enough children, add stuffed animals or Lego people.)
- Genesis 6:5 poster

Background: After Abel's death, Cain left his parents to live in another part of the world. Adam and Eve had another son, Seth. Years went by, and the population grew. People began to spread across the land. As more and more people were born, they forgot about the God who had created them.

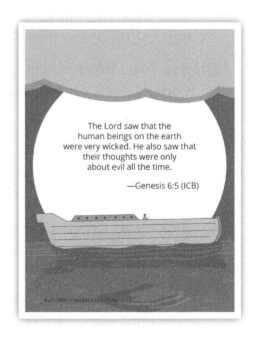

The Lord saw that the human beings on the earth were very wicked. He also saw that their thoughts were only about evil all the time.

—Genesis 6:5 (ICB)

BIBLE AND OBJECT LESSON

■ ■

{Hold up the bag of water. Choose a child to come to the front and hold the bag straight out in front of himself. Have him stay there while you tell the story. Read Genesis 6:5-10 aloud.}

{Ask:}

- How wicked had people become? [*All of their thoughts were evil all the time.*]

- How did God feel about the people? [*He regretted that He had made human beings; His heart was troubled.*]

- Who found favor with God? [*Noah*]

- Why? [*Noah was a righteous man and blameless among the people; he walked faithfully with God.*]

- How many sons did Noah have? [*Three*]

- Does the Bible say that Noah's sons had found favor with God? [*No*]

{Choose four boys to represent Noah and his sons. Have them stand along the front. Check on the water holder to be sure that the water is still in the air.}

Here are Noah and his sons. God saw Noah as a righteous man living among people who lived sinful, violent lives. We do not know much about his sons, but the Bible does not tell us that they were righteous.

{Read Genesis 6:13-14 and 17-19.}

{Ask:}

- Why was God going to destroy the people and the earth? [*The people were evil all the time; the earth was filled with violence.*]

- What did He tell Noah to do? [*Make an ark, a large boat*]

- Of what was the ark made? [*Cypress wood coated with pitch (tar) inside and out*]

- What was the purpose of the floodwaters? [*They would destroy life under the heavens; everything on earth was to perish.*]
- BUT what was God going to do? [*He was going to establish a covenant between Himself and Noah.*]
- What is a covenant? [*An agreement between God and His people*]
- Who was on the ark? [*All who wanted to come. Noah, his wife, his three sons and their wives—eight people.*]

{Choose four girls to represent the women on the ark. Ask:}

- Do you see everyone else in the room? What happens to us? [*We would be destroyed by floodwaters.*]

2 Peter 2:5 tells us that Noah preached righteousness to those around him. Therefore, all of the people were encouraged to repent and get right with God before the Flood occurred.

{Have the eight children sit. Read Genesis 6:20-22 and 7:2-4.}

{Ask:}

- Did Noah go and find all of the animals? [*No, they came to him.*]
- How many animals of each kind came to Noah? [*Two of each kind, male and female*]
- What else did Noah do besides build the ark? [*Gathered and stored food*]
- Was Noah obedient? [*Yes*]

{Read Genesis 7:2-4.}

- How many of each clean animal (sheep, cattle, goats, doves, etc.) were going to be saved by the ark? [*Seven pairs of each—14 of each*]

- How many days were left until God would destroy the earth? [*Seven*]

- **{Speak to the child with the water. Take the water from him.}** How's your arm? It's only been a few minutes. Is your arm tired? [*Yes*]

- How long did God say He would send rain? [*40 days and nights*]

- Can water do some mighty things during that time? [*Yes*]

There is only a little bit of water in this bag. It's enough to make your arm tired. It's enough to drink. It's enough to wash away some dirt. Think about big storms. Hurricanes usually last one to two days as they travel over land, leaving destruction in their path. Imagine how damaged and changed the earth would be after 40 days! And what would happen to all of the dead bodies of the people and the animals? It was a terrible time! It broke God's heart to destroy what He had created.

It rained for 40 days. If you keep reading in Genesis, you figure out that Noah and his family were floating around on the ark for about 9½ months. Once the waters receded and the ark landed on Mt. Ararat, God told Noah they could all come out.

{Read Genesis 8:20-21 and 9:13-17.}

- What is a covenant? [*An agreement between God and His people*]

- What is God's promise? [*He will never send a flood to destroy all life again.*]

- Does this mean we will never see floods? [*No. We will have local floods, but not a world-wide flood.*]

- What is the symbol of this promise? [*A rainbow*]

God is now doing what He promised He would do. In fact, He says the word over and over. When God repeats something, we need to stop and take notice.

LIFE APPLICATION

■ ■

God takes sin seriously, but He always has a remnant. This is an important truth that is told throughout the Old Testament. God will find those who are righteous. They are righteous because of His grace. God will use righteous people to work His plan.

Noah was surrounded by people who were against God. Regardless, Noah preached repentance. Noah was righteous in God's eyes. Noah walked with God. He was different. He stood out. He was probably mocked, laughed at, and ignored. I'm sure it was hard to face people being mean.

The story of Noah is a great picture of Jesus. Everyone born on this earth is born into sin. All have sinned. We all deserve to be destroyed because God is holy and cannot have anything to do with sin.

The ark saved Noah and his family from destruction. Jesus saves those who believe in Him from eternal destruction. Those who choose to believe in Him will not perish but will have eternal life. God is a God of grace.

However, there is one difference between Noah's event and ours. Noah's sons were not found to be righteous, but they were saved anyway because they were Noah's sons. When it comes to believing in Jesus as your Savior, you must decide for yourself. Just because your mom or dad believes in Jesus does not mean that you do. You must decide on your own to follow Jesus.

If you choose to believe in Jesus and let Him guide your life, please understand that you may be mocked, laughed at, or ignored. We are told to be different. Those who are righteous do not blend in with the society around them. Those who are walking with God do not walk in behaviors that mock or ignore the God who saved them. People who claim to believe in Jesus try to act like Jesus.

What if you know a person who says he believes in Jesus but does not act like it? Start asking questions. That's what Jesus did. Jesus would ask people questions to get them thinking about their behavior. You can do the same thing.

What can we learn from Noah and the Flood? Sin is a serious matter. All people need a Savior. If we choose to believe Jesus has saved us, then we must understand that others might not treat us well. However, Noah remained righteous and we can, too.

COMMENT BOX

████████████████████████████████████

THINK: What went well as you taught this lesson? What can you do better?

_____

_____

_____

_____

_____

_____

_____

_____

_____

TIP: This object lesson worked well with 3rd-6th graders. For the K-2nd graders, I chose to hold the water myself and just have eight children stand and then sit down.

5 THE TOWER OF BABEL

■ ■

Why are there so many languages if all people came from Noah's family? Where did Ham, Shem, and Japheth end up living? And why should we care about this today? The Tower of Babel is more relevant than you might think.

Scripture Focus: Genesis 11:1-9

Materials:

- Language cards (See **Resources Page**. Print one copy on paper or cardstock; cut the cards apart.)
- Genesis 11:7 poster

Background: Noah's family was saved from destruction by using the ark. After the water receded and the ark rested on top of Mt. Ararat, God placed the rainbow in the sky as a sign of His covenant to never destroy humanity with a world-wide flood again. God also told Noah and his family to multiply and spread out over the earth.

FUTUREFLYINGSAUCERS.COM

Come, let us go down and confuse their language. Then they will not be able to understand each other.

—Genesis 11:7 (ICB)

OBJECT LESSON

■ ■

{Once you have the cards cut apart, put them in a stack from hardest to easiest to figure out what the words mean. For example, I speak English, so that would be last. Chinese, Hebrew, or Russian would be first. Hold up each card and have the children figure out the message.}

I have a stack of cards that have a message. I'm going to hold them up one at a time, and you tell me what they say.

{The children will respond strongly to the languages that are very different from their own. Make this a fun activity!}

{Ask:}

- How are these languages different? [*Some use pictures. Some use symbols we have never seen before. Others use the same letters we use.*]

- How are these language cards the same? [*They all have the same message: Jesus is Lord!*]

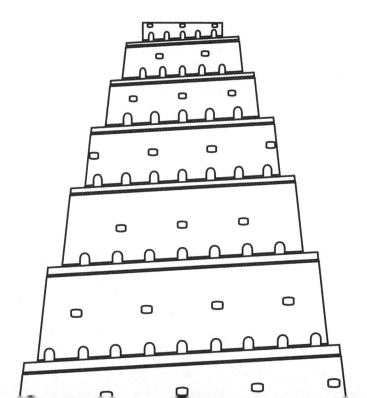

BIBLE LESSON

{Put the cards to the side.}

After the Flood, God told Noah and his family to multiply and fill the earth. Babies grew up and had babies, and more and more children were born, but they did not spread out. Instead, they moved to a place called the Plain of Shinar. No one really knows exactly where that was located, but it might have been between the Tigris and Euphrates Rivers.

The people decided to create bricks and build a city. Not only did they want to build a city, but they wanted to build a tower. The Bible tells us that they wanted to build a tower that would have a top in the heavens. The people wanted to make a name for themselves. They were prideful.

{Ask:}

- Do you like to be remembered? [*Yes*]
- Tell me some examples of times when you were remembered by someone. [*Allow for answers. Answers might include being invited to a birthday party, being left at the grocery store and someone coming to pick them up, being left at school, someone remembering the child was sick, etc.*]

The people wanted to be remembered, but it was more than that. God knows our hearts. He knew what was going on in the hearts of those people who were building the city and the tower. God went down to the city to watch what they were doing.

Scripture tells us that God recognized that the people were of one accord. They had one language. When people begin to desire power over obedience to God, they become dangerous to themselves and others.

Therefore, God confused the language of the people. They stopped building, and the Lord scattered them all over the earth.

{Ask:}

- Why would God want all of the people to be scattered on the earth? [*Allow for answers. Lead conversation to include the idea that in places where there are many people crowded together, there is often more crime and tragedy. God wants to take care of His people and protect them.*]

- Does this mean that large cities are bad places in which to live? [*No. But there are certain qualities of life that people think about when choosing a place to live.*]

- Once people began speaking in these different languages, where did they go? [*Allow for predictions.*]

We have to go back a chapter to Genesis 10. It's a genealogy chapter. It also tells us how people united as nations and divided by languages. Remember, Noah had three sons: Ham, Shem, and Japheth. Because God is not a god of chaos, it makes sense that He would scatter people in an organized way. And He did.

People scattered in family units called clans, and each clan had their own language. The descendants of Ham are thought to be the people of Egypt, Ethiopia, North Africa, and Canaan. The people in Europe and western Asia are thought to have come from Japheth. Shem is ten generations away from a man named Abram, and the Hebrew people are from his line.

LIFE APPLICATION

■ ■

{Show the cards of the different languages and ask:}

• Why do different languages matter to us today? [*Allow for answers.*]

When Jesus was here on the earth, He told the disciples to go into all the nations and make disciples. Those who love Jesus are still doing that today. There are still people groups who have not heard about Jesus. They do not know the gospel. They do not know about salvation.

Revelation 5:9 tells us about a song that is sung in heaven, and the words tell us that those who are redeemed come from every **tribe, tongue, people, and nation**.

{Ask:}

• Does this leave any people group out? [*No*]

• Yet, does this verse leave any people out? [*Yes, those who are not redeemed by Jesus*]

God spread people across the earth beginning with the Tower of Babel. When Jesus returns, there will be people who represent every tribe and nation. All of those people will be saying the message on our cards in their own language.

{Ask:}

• What is the message on these cards? [*Jesus is Lord!*]

What can we learn from the Tower of Babel? We are to be disciples who help share the gospel with those of every nation and tongue. That might mean going to other nations, or it might mean talking with our neighbors across the street. But all of those who love Jesus must obey His command to make disciples.

COMMENT BOX

■ ■ ■ ■ ■ ■ ■ ■ ■ ■ ■ ■ ■ ■ ■ ■ ■ ■ ■ ■

THINK: What went well as you taught this lesson? What can you do better?

_____

_____

_____

_____

_____

_____

_____

_____

_____

TIP: If you are teaching multiple groups at different times, be sure to number the cards so you know in what order to put them for the next lesson.

6 THE CALL OF ABRAM

■ ■

Promises. We all make them. We all break many of them. Yet God has made hundreds of promises to us, and not once has He broken them. Trusting that God will be Who He says He is, and that He will do what He says He is going to do, is vital to our foundation of faith. This object lesson on the call of Abram and his flight to Egypt will encourage children to trust in the One True God.

Scripture Focus: Genesis 12

Materials:

- A deck of playing cards (Have the cards separated by books. Take out the jokers.)
- Genesis 12:1 poster

Geography: Fertile Crescent, Ur, Haran, and the land of Canaan

Then the Lord said to Abram, "Leave your country, your relatives and your father's family. Go to the land I will show you."

—Genesis 12:1 (ICB)

FUTUREFLYINGSAUCERS.COM

Background: After the Tower of Babel, the people spread out across the land. About eight generations after Shem, Terah was born. Terah's sons were Abram, Nahor, and Haran. Haran died and left his son, Lot. Abram's wife was Sarai, and she was barren. Abram's father, Terah, moved his family from Ur to Haran, and at 205 years old, he died. It was in Haran that God approached Abram with a promise.

OBJECT LESSON

■ ■

{Fan the cards in front of you, showing the backs of the cards to the children.}

{Ask:}

- Do you know how to play Go Fish? [*Allow for answers. Each player gets five cards. The rest of the deck is placed in the middle of the players.*]

- When you play Go Fish, you try to collect books of cards. Who can explain what a book is? [*Allow for answers. The goal is for each player to win "books" which are comprised of the same number from each suit (for example, all four 2 cards).*]

- Let us say I ask you to play Go Fish with me, but we MUST use MY deck of cards. Would you be ok with that? [*Allow for answers, but they should say yes.*]

{Place the stack of cards face down in front of you.}

You are I start playing the game. Soon you notice that I am winning lots of books. You also notice that as soon as you draw a card, I ask for the same card.

{Ask:}

- What do you think might be causing me to win so easily? [*Allow for answers, but they should figure out that cheating is happening.*]

When people play cards, there is a way to cheat called "stacking the deck." **{Turn the deck over and spread out the cards so the children can see all of the cards already in books.}** The cheater manipulates the cards so that the opponent loses. The one who is cheating at the card game doesn't trust the cards. He doesn't trust that he will win fairly.

{Ask:}

- Will you win every game you play? [*No*]

- When you obey God, will you always be successful? [*Allow for answers. We may not be successful in the world's eyes, or even in our own. But obedience ALWAYS wins with God.*]

BIBLE LESSON

■ ■

A man named Abram lived in Haran. His wife's name was Sarai. They had no children. One day God spoke to Abram. The Bible does not tell us why God chose to talk with Abram. In fact, Joshua 24:2 tells us that Abram's father, Terah, and Abram served other gods. We do learn later on in Hebrews that Abram had faith in the Lord, as did Sarai.

The Lord told Abram to do a hard thing. God told Abram to leave his family and go to a strange land. He then made some promises to Abram.

God told Abram that:

- He would lead Abram to a **land.**
- He would make of Abram a great **nation.**
- Abram would have a great **name.**
- **All families** of the earth would be **blessed**.

{Use the bold words to create a list to help memorize the four-fold promise of God to Abram. These four things are important to remember. Go over the list with the children three or four times.}

Abram obeyed God and left Haran. He was 75 years old. Sarai and Lot went with him. They traveled, and God led them to the land of Canaan. There God appeared to Abram and told him that this was the land He would be giving to Abram's descendants. Abram settled there and called on the name of the Lord...

...Until there was a famine. Abram went to Egypt. Before they entered Egypt, Abram told Sarai to tell the Egyptians that she was his sister instead of his wife. Abram knew that she was beautiful; he knew that Pharaoh would want her as a wife and would kill him. Abram was right. Pharaoh did want Sarai and he did take her. But because he was told that Sarai was Abram's sister, Pharaoh treated Abram well and gave him many things.

Suddenly Pharaoh and his house were plagued. The Bible does not tell us what the plagues were, but I'm sure they were bad. In Egypt, the people believed that everything happened because of their gods. So when this plague happened,

Pharaoh probably went to his temples first. Eventually he and the priests figured out that the plague started when Sarai entered his home.

Pharaoh confronted Abram. He gave Sarai back to him before Pharaoh had touched her, and he told them to leave Egypt.

LIFE APPLICATION

■ ■

{Ask:}

- Is God trustworthy? [*Yes*]

- Does God do what He says He is going to do? [*Yes*]

- What did God promise Abram? [*Land, nation, name, and all families will be blessed*]

- So far in Genesis, which part of the promise has God brought about? [*He took Abram to the land.*]

- Is there more to do? [*Yes*]

- When Abram went to Egypt, did he trust God to care for him? [*No, he lied and had Sarai lie.*]

- Abram tried to manipulate Pharaoh because he thought he would be killed. What should Abram have done? [*Told the truth and allowed God to take care of the situation*]

- If God's promise wasn't completed yet, did Abram need to worry about Pharaoh killing him? [*No, Abram needed to trust God.*]

When God tells us to do something and we choose to obey Him, God is not going to turn His back on us. He will provide everything we need to be successful in His mission. Things might look troublesome in our eyes, but if we are trusting God, He is going to help us.

God made a promise to Abram and it had not been fulfilled yet. There was no need for Abram to manipulate the situation and sin in order to save his life. God would have helped him. There is no need for us to "stack the cards" so we can win a game. We don't need to cheat or lie when we are obeying God. **Lying is sin, and God will never ask you to sin.**

The fourth part of the promise given to Abram has to do with us. We are those families that will be blessed. Jesus is one of Abram's descendants, and He is the one who blesses all families with the gift of salvation.

What can we learn from the call of Abram? When God asks us to do something and we choose to obey, then He will help us to be successful in His power.

COMMENT BOX

■ ■

THINK: What went well as you taught this lesson? What can you do better?

_____

_____

_____

_____

_____

_____

_____

_____

_____

TIP: The four parts of the promise are essential to understanding what God does throughout the rest of the Old Testament. Be sure to review them with the children often.

7 ABRAHAM'S CHALLENGE TO SACRIFICE ISAAC

■ ■

Sacrifice. It isn't something people like to talk about, let alone do. This lesson based upon God's command for Abraham to sacrifice Isaac will help children understand the meaning of sacrifice and why God asks us to be a living sacrifice.

Scripture Focus: Genesis 17:1-7, 15-16; 22:1-19

Materials:

- Small model or picture of a ram

- Gold, black, red, and white construction paper (or a Wordless Book)

- Genesis 22:13b

Geography: Canaan

Background: God promised that He would 1) give Abram land; 2) turn his family into a great nation; 3) make his name great; and 4) bless all the families of the world through him. God made a blood covenant with Himself, promising these things to Abram.

So Abraham went and took the sheep and killed it. He offered it as a whole burnt offering to God. Abraham's son was saved.

—Genesis 22:13b (ICB)

OBJECT LESSON

■ ■

{Hold up the model sheep or ram and ask:}

- What is this? [*A sheep/ram*]

- What do we know about sheep and the Old Testament? [*Allow for answers. Be sure that sacrificing in the Temple or on altars is mentioned. See the Tip for this lesson for an extra lesson on the Tabernacle.*]

- Why were sheep slaughtered and burned for sacrifices? [*God told the Hebrews to sacrifice the sheep for sins. The sheep took the place of the people. The wages of sin is death (Romans 6:23). Something or someone must die.*]

BIBLE LESSON

■ ■

Abram and Sarai left everything they knew to follow God's directions. He took them to a new land that would eventually be used for their descendants. Abram was 75 years old when he left Haran. As part of the promise, God told Abram that he would have descendants. The only way for that to happen was for Sarai to have a baby. Twenty-four years went by. Abram still did not have a son.

God appeared to Abram and spoke the promise again. God also changed Abram's name to Abraham because he was to be the father of many nations. Then God changed Sarai's name to Sarah because she was to be the mother of many nations. At this, Abraham questioned God, because he was 99 years old and Sarah was 90. But God assured Abraham that Sarah would have a son.

A year later Sarah had a son, and he was named Isaac. Isaac grew into a boy and then a young man.

{Read Genesis 22:1-19. Remind the children that this Old Testament account happened thousands of years before Jesus came to earth. Read it again and point out the parallels between this event and Jesus' crucifixion. These parallels include:}

- Abraham's only son = God's only Son
- Saddled a donkey to ride = Jesus rode a donkey into Jerusalem
- Two young men went with them = two thieves on the crosses
- Arrived on the third day = resurrected on the third day
- Isaac carried the wood = Jesus carried the wooden cross
- Bound Isaac and laid him on the altar = Jesus nailed to the cross
- Ram caught in the thicket by the horns = the crown of thorns on Jesus' head
- Ram replaced Isaac as the sacrifice = Jesus took our place and was the sacrifice for our sins
- Place called "The Lord Will Provide" = God provided His own Son
- Because Abraham obeyed, he was blessed = When we obey God, we are blessed.

Through this testing, Abraham and Isaac are "acting out" the crucifixion and salvation experience to some degree. God is asking Abraham to sacrifice his son, his one and only son. Abraham's faith now is quite different from his lack of faith when he went to Egypt during the famine.

The book of Hebrews tells us that Abraham's faith was strong. He had concluded that if God had promised to give him Isaac, and that all of the other blessings were to come through him, therefore God must raise Isaac from the dead. What a difference compared to the fear Abraham had in Egypt!

LIFE APPLICATION

■ ■

Even though Abraham knew nothing about Jesus, he did know God. Abraham did not know the Ten Commandments either, because they came hundreds of years later. Romans 4:3 tells us that Abraham believed God, and then righteousness was given to him.

For those of us after the Old Testament, we do know about Jesus. We are to tell others about Jesus. For us, our righteousness comes through believing in Jesus.

{Proceed through the Wordless Book.}

{Show the gold page.} Describe God. God is holy, glorious, and perfect.

{Show the black page.} Describe people. We are dark with sin. We cannot have a relationship with God because of this sin. All of us have fallen short of the glory of God. We are like Isaac. We must die because of sin. BUT...

{Show the red page.} God sent a substitute for us! Just like the ram was substituted for Isaac, Jesus takes our place. The wages of sin is death.

{Hold up the ram.} Instead of us having to die, God sent JESUS to die and take our place. Jesus is the One who fixes the sin problem that we have. If we believe in the Lord Jesus, then instead of God seeing us dirty with sin...

{Show the white page.} He sees us as being clean and righteous, like Abraham was because of his faith in God. The Bible tells us that if we believe on the Lord Jesus, then we will be saved. That is one of God's promises. Would you like to be white as snow? Would you like all that sin to be washed away?

Once you decide to believe in Jesus, He makes you righteous before God. Now you can live a life walking around like a living sacrifice, because Jesus died in your place. A person who is a living sacrifice is one who tries to think, say, and do what Jesus would do. This is the opposite of someone who stays in their sin. A living sacrifice dies to self. We put our wants and desires to the side and put others first.

What can we learn from Abraham and Isaac? God sent His Son, His only Son, to earth. Jesus was divine and sinless, but He took our place and died on the cross. He rose three days later. His death allows us to live.

COMMENT BOX

■ ■

THINK: What went well as you taught this lesson? What can you do better?

_____

_____

_____

_____

_____

_____

_____

_____

_____

TIP: You may find that the children have no idea about Old Testament sacrifices. For a bonus lesson, see the Resources Page for a Tabernacle lesson that explains more about this topic.

JACOB AND ESAU

Sin always hurts. It might be fun or pretty at first, but sin always hurts. It will harm you, and it might harm others. This object lesson based on the manipulation of Jacob and Esau will help children understand that choosing forgiveness and Jesus is better than choosing the ways of sin.

Scripture Focus: Genesis 27

Materials:

- Sunglasses
- Genesis 27:30 poster

Geography: Canaan

Background: Abraham had passed the four-part covenant on to Isaac, and now Isaac is prepared to pass it on to Esau. Covenants, or blessings, were passed through the generations by the father giving a blessing to the oldest son. Inheritances were passed on this way, as well. This gave the oldest son legal authority over the family. Isaac had two sons, Esau and Jacob.

Isaac finished blessing Jacob. Then, just as Jacob left his father Isaac, Esau came in from hunting.

—Genesis 27:30 (ICB)

OBJECT LESSON

■ ■

{Put sunglasses on as kids arrive. Describe what you cannot see. Pretend you cannot read the Bible well. You can be silly with this! The kids will enjoy telling you that you have sunglasses on. Ask:}

- Why can't I see well? [*You have sunglasses on inside.*]

- But if I can see fine outside with them on, why can't I use them inside? [*It's too dark inside to use them.*]

{Take sunglasses off.} I can see so much better now! Your faces were hidden and distorted. I couldn't read very well. It was too dark and I couldn't see things as they really were. Now that the glasses are off, I can see pretty colors and details that I was not able to see before.

This is what sin does to us. Sin distorts and deceives us into thinking we know the Truth. Sin blocks our vision. If we are looking at Truth through sunglasses, we are going to miss how wonderful the Truth really is. Not only can we be deceived by our own sin, but we can also be deceived by the sins of others.

BIBLE LESSON

Isaac was old, and he knew he didn't have many days left to live. He was blind. Isaac knew he needed to pass on the inheritance and blessing to his oldest son, Esau. Isaac told Esau to go hunt and make Isaac's favorite meal. Then Esau was to bring the meal to Isaac, who would then bless him after he ate. Esau left, but someone had overheard the conversation.

Rebekah, Esau's mother, went to Jacob, her younger son, and told him what conversation had taken place.

{Put on the sunglasses.} She wanted Jacob to have the blessing because he was her favorite son. She told Jacob to go kill a goat and fix a meal to take to Isaac.

{Take off the glasses.} Jacob was concerned because Esau was a hunter and was hairy. Jacob didn't look or smell anything like his brother.

{Put on the sunglasses.} Rebekah had a plan. She took the skins of the goat and put them on Jacob, and then she dressed him in Esau's clothing.

Now Jacob was dressed up like his brother. He was about to go and deceive his father.

Jacob went to his father's tent and told him that he had brought the meal for him to eat. Isaac was confused.

{Take off the glasses.} Esau was back too soon, and the voice Isaac heard sounded like Jacob. *"Is it really you?"*

{Put on the sunglasses.} *"Yes, my father!"*

Jacob went closer and allowed Isaac to feel the lamb's wool on his arms and neck, and let him smell the clothes. Isaac took the food and ate it. Afterwards, Isaac blessed Jacob.

{Take off sunglasses.} At this point, the blessing and inheritance went to Jacob, NOT Esau. The younger son stole the birthright and blessing from the oldest son.

Jacob left. Esau arrived. *"I brought your meal, Father!"*

"What? Who are you?"

"Your son, Esau!"

{Put on the sunglasses; then take them off very slowly.} Isaac, who was blind, realized what had happened. His "eyes" were opened to the Truth. The sins of Rebekah and Jacob were found out.

Isaac said, *"I have already given the blessing to your brother!"*

Esau wept bitterly and begged his father for a blessing. Isaac gave him one, but it was not nearly as great of the one Jacob had received.

When Esau left, he vowed to himself that once his father died, he would kill Jacob for stealing his birthright and inheritance from him.

Rebekah was told of Esau's rage, and she had Jacob leave the country to go live with her brother, Laban.

LIFE APPLICATION

■ ■

{Put on the sunglasses.} Sin. Sin is why we need to know the Bible. The Bible tells us what type of behaviors and attitudes are sinful. **Reading the Bible helps us to take the sunglasses off our hearts so we can see God's Truth.**

The goal is to take the sunglasses off and keep them off. **{Take the glasses off.}** But there are times when we CHOOSE to put the glasses on. **{Put on the sunglasses.}** And that's not pleasing to the Lord. Staying in sin and choosing to sin is not what God wants for His children. He wants us to walk in the Truth because Jesus is the Truth. **{Take the glasses off.}**

Whether we choose to sin, or we accidentally do the wrong thing, we should choose to mend the relationships with others and with God. Believing in Jesus and asking the Father to forgive us when we sin are the first actions we should take. Next, we need to ask the person whom we wronged to forgive us. It was years before Jacob would reconcile with his brother and father.

What can we learn from Jacob and Esau? Sometimes we accidentally sin. Other times we purposely choose to sin. But all sin can be forgiven through Christ Jesus.

COMMENT BOX

■ ■

THINK: What went well as you taught this lesson? What can you do better?

_____

_____

_____

_____

_____

_____

_____

_____

_____

TIP: If you have enough, supply sunglasses for all the children after the lesson. Have them discuss ways they sin. Have them put on the sunglasses for each sin. When discussing what Scripture says, have them remove the glasses.

JACOB WRESTLES WITH GOD

■ ■

Wrestling with God. Fighting with God. Everyone does it. Everyone will encounter God at some point in their lives. This object lesson about Jacob wrestling with God will help children understand that we must surrender our sinful lives so we can be blessed with eternal life.

Scripture Focus: Genesis 32

Materials:

- Container
- Water
- Cornstarch
- Towels
- Genesis 32:26 poster

Then the man said to Jacob,
"Let me go. The sun is coming up."
But Jacob said,
"I will let you go if you will bless me."

—Genesis 32:26 (ICB)

{To make oobleck: Use 1 cup of water to 1½–2 cups of cornstarch. Put the water in the container. Slowly add the cornstarch. Mixing can be tricky. Oobleck has properties of both solids and liquids. If you punch it, it feels solid. If you touch it gently, your hand will sink into the material. Add cornstarch until you can do this. You'll probably have to mix with your hands.}

Geography: Jabbok River, land of Israel

Background: Jacob has been in Haran at his Uncle Laban's house for 20 years. Jacob now has 2 wives and 11 children. While many men in the Bible had more

53

than one wife, it was not something that honored God. In fact, having more than one wife usually caused trouble in the home.

Jacob is extremely nervous about meeting his brother after tricking him years before.

Names are very important in the Bible. Many times, parents chose to wait a few days to give their children names. Names were to reflect the person's character or personality. Jacob's name meant "deceiver." When in a battle, it was a form of surrender to state your name to the opposition.

OBJECT LESSON

■ ■

{Open the container of oobleck. Shake it slightly and ask:}

- What is this stuff? Is this a liquid? [*The kids may already be familiar with oobleck. Continue to describe the characteristics of the material as you punch it and pick it up, allowing it to dribble from your hand. If you have a small number of students, allow them to manipulate it.*]

Oobleck can be described as a solid AND a liquid. It can be either hard or runny, but it is still called oobleck. If you punch it, it seems to be solid. If you scoop some into your hand, the oobleck softens and pours out.

BIBLE LESSON

{For older children, have them read Genesis 32:3-32.}

Jacob, the deceiver, was on his way home from Haran. While at Uncle Laban's house, he had acquired great wealth, but he was still scared to face his past. He had sent scouts to see if Esau was near. They returned and told him that Esau was going to meet him with 400 men.

Jacob was scared. He prayed to God to deliver him from Esau. When he reached the Jabbok River, Jacob sent a huge gift of camels, donkeys, cows, and sheep on ahead to Esau in the hopes that it might soften Esau's heart toward him. Then Jacob decided to send his wives and children over the river to meet Esau, hoping that they would soften Esau's heart as well. He was going to follow behind. He was acting like a coward.

Jacob stayed behind as night fell. He was alone. Then a Man appeared and wrestled with Jacob. Jacob wrestled until morning. When the Man saw that Jacob was not going to quit, He touched Jacob's hip socket and made it fall out of joint. Jacob wrestled on. The Man said, *"Let me go!"*

Jacob, who probably knew by now Who the Man was, replied, *"Not until You bless me!"*

The Man asked, *"What is your name?"*

At this point Jacob surrendered. *"Jacob."* (Jacob means "Deceiver.")

The Man replied, *"Your name shall no longer be Jacob, but Israel!"* (Israel means "God fights" or "One who strives with God.")

This was a life-changing event for Jacob, and so he renamed the place where this encounter took place. He named it *Peniel* because he had seen God face to face, and his life was spared.

Jacob limped across the river and then moved to the front of the family and possessions. He was a changed man. Jacob met Esau first, instead of going behind his family. Esau ran to Jacob and they both wept, kissed, and hugged. Jacob walked with a limp the rest of his life.

LIFE APPLICATION

■ ■ ■ ■ ■ ■ ■ ■ ■ ■ ■ ■ ■ ■ ■ ■ ■ ■

This physical event in Jacob's life reflects the spiritual events in our lives.

{Ask:}

- What was Jacob doing? [*Returning to the land of his father. Genesis 31:3)*]
- What was he feeling? Why? [*He was scared because he had tricked Esau out of the blessing and birthright. Esau had wanted to kill him*.]
- What did Jacob pray? [*Lord, deliver me.*]
- What does this mean? [*Save me.*]

Jacob was greatly afraid because he had stolen the blessing and birthright from Esau. Jacob had been his own master instead of allowing God to give him the blessing. He knew that Esau wanted to kill him. You are born into sin. You like to be your own master. However, at some point you will recognize that you aren't perfect or in charge of life, and that can make you afraid. Jacob prayed to God, asking Him to deliver him—to save him. People pray to God when they are scared. Maybe you have, too. We want Him to save us from what is happening.

{Ask:}

- When did a Man come and fight Jacob? [*At night when Jacob was alone*]
- What did the Man want Jacob to do, and how did Jacob respond? [*The Man wanted him to let go, and Jacob told Him he wouldn't let go until He blessed him.*]
- What did the Man do to Jacob? [*Touched his hip socket and made him go lame*]

Jacob was alone in the dark. At some point, you must understand that your life is your own. Your decisions are your own. You don't live for your parents, or a brother or sister, or a friend. Your life is your life. Your sin is your sin. Jacob wrestled with a Man and would not let go until he was blessed. If you haven't already, you will encounter God. He will call you to Himself. You can either wrestle with Him, or you can walk away.

Jesus is holy, perfect, and powerful. You are sinful and broken. When you are your own master, then you are fighting against God.

{Ask:}

- How did the Man bless Jacob? [*He gave him the new name of Israel*.]
- What happened when the sun rose? [*Jacob crossed the river*.]

The Man asked Jacob his name at the end of the fight. Jacob told his name in surrender. When you ask God to forgive you and confess your sins to Him, then you are recognizing that God is in charge. You surrender to Him. Jesus becomes your Master.

The Man gave Jacob a new name, *Israel*, which means "God fights." When you encounter Jesus, believing that He saves you from your sin, and you confess with your mouth that He is Lord, He turns you into a new creation.

The sun rose, and Jacob crossed over into the Promised Land. Jesus is the Light of the World. When you believe in Him, you enter eternal life. You don't go to heaven right away, but you get to live a life worthy of Jesus.

{Ask:}

- What did Jacob call the place where he wrestled with the Man? [*Peniel, which means "I have seen God face to face, and my life is spared."*]
- Did Jacob's hip ever heal? [*No, he walked with a limp*.]
- Did Jacob make peace with Esau? [*Yes, read a little into chapter 33*.]
- Who do you think the "Man" was? [*No one really knows. It could have been an angel, but because of what Jacob names the place, I think he wrestled with Jesus*.]

Jacob named the place *Peniel* because he had seen God face to face and his life had been protected. When you are saved from your sin, write down the date because that was when you encountered God and He protected your life from eternal death.

Jacob limped for the rest of his life. Once you are saved from sin and have God as your Master, you will still sin. However, "God fights" for you, and the Holy Spirit will guide you if you listen. You can overcome sin and temptation and become more like Jesus.

{Show the oobleck.}

This oobleck can be hard and solid, but when I pick it up, it becomes flexible in my hand. It changes. When we encounter God, we have hard hearts and we want to be totally in charge of our lives. But if we allow God to touch us, He will change us. Like Jacob, we will never be the same again. If we stay in the hand of God and listen to the Holy Spirit, then our lives will bring much joy and pleasure to God, ourselves, and others. Instead of being hard-hearted, in God's hand we become usable, flexible, and able to glorify God.

What can we learn from Jacob? Each person will encounter God at some point. If we surrender to Him, then we will be blessed.

COMMENT BOX

THINK: What went well as you taught this lesson? What can you do better?

_____

_____

_____

_____

_____

_____

_____

_____

TIP: Oobleck can be messy, especially if you allow the kids to play with it. Put a tablecloth on the ground, and have a sink nearby to wash hands.

10   JOSEPH

■■■■■■■■■■■■■■■■■■■■■■

God makes many promises in the Bible. Sometimes we are so busy that we miss them. Sometimes we expect those promises to happen quickly, in our time. God doesn't work that way, though. He makes wonderful promises and fulfills them when HE wants them to happen. This object lesson about Joseph will help your children understand that they can still be lights in the darkness, even when God is not in a hurry.

Scripture Focus: Genesis 37-47 [*This is a lot of Scripture, but to show that God works in His time for His glory, we need to see the big picture of Joseph's life. If you teach older children and have the time to read it all, split the reading between them. For younger children, paraphrase the content.*]

Materials:

- Flashlight
- Dark-colored washcloth or towel
- Genesis 45:7 poster

Geography: Canaan, Egypt, and Goshen

Background: Abraham had passed the four-part covenant on to Isaac, who passed it on to Jacob.

So God sent me here ahead of you. This was to make sure you have some descendants left on earth. And it was to keep you alive in an amazing way.

—Genesis 45:7 (ICB)

FUTUREFLYINGSAUCERS.COM

Jacob's name was changed to Israel. Jacob was the father of 12 sons. Abraham, Isaac, and Jacob are known as the Patriarchs of the Jewish nation of Israel.

During all these years, Egypt had combined the Upper and Lower kingdoms to create one nation of Egypt.

BIBLE AND OBJECT LESSON

■ ■ ■ ■ ■ ■ ■ ■ ■ ■ ■ ■ ■ ■ ■ ■ ■ ■ ■ ■

{Turn on the flashlight. Ask:}

- What can you tell me about light? [*It shines. We can see with it. It's not dark.*]

- What would happen if I try to cover it up? [*The light will not shine as brightly.*]

{Put the washcloth over the lens. Ask:}

- Can you still see the light? [*It isn't as bright, but yes, the light can still be seen.*]

Jacob had 12 sons. The eleventh son's name was Joseph, and God used him in a powerful way. In everything Joseph did, he allowed God to shine through him, even when he went through darker, tougher times.

The history of Joseph is interesting because he's one of the only people we learn about from his childhood until his death. It is important to note that Scripture tells us that Jacob loved Joseph more than the other brothers. Because he loved him more, Jacob treated Joseph differently. When Joseph was young, he made some unwise choices in his relationship with his family, especially with his brothers. Joseph was a sinner, just like you and me.

Here are the main events that happen in Joseph's life:

{As you go through the life of Joseph, shine the flashlight bright during the times when God was near to Joseph. Cover the light when God seems far away and bad things happened.}

- Joseph gave a bad report about his brothers to his father.

- Joseph had dreams; he told his brothers and father.

- His brothers were jealous and hated Joseph.

- Joseph was given a coat of many colors because his father, Jacob, loved him more than the others.

- The brothers were tending sheep; Joseph went to check on them.

- The brothers plotted to kill Joseph; Reuben had the idea of putting Joseph in a pit instead.

- Judah had the idea to sell Joseph to traders; they did, and they took the colored coat with animal blood on it to Jacob.

- Joseph was sold as a slave in Egypt to Potiphar; **Joseph was blessed** because God was with him.

- Potiphar's wife falsely accused Joseph and he went to jail.

- **Joseph was blessed** because the Lord was with him; he was given leadership of the other prisoners.

- Pharaoh's baker and cup-bearer were put in jail; they had dreams. **Joseph interpreted the dreams correctly.**

- The cupbearer forgot about Joseph.

- Pharaoh had a dream; **Joseph was remembered.**

- **Joseph interpreted the dream; Joseph became second in command of all Egypt.**

- Famine came; Joseph's brothers came to Egypt for food.

- **Joseph forgave them;** Jacob and the family moved to Egypt and lived in the land of Goshen.

LIFE APPLICATION

■ ■ ■ ■ ■ ■ ■ ■ ■ ■ ■ ■ ■ ■ ■ ■ ■ ■ ■

Once he was sold into slavery, Joseph needed to grow up quickly. He made better choices. He relied on God. Joseph allowed his light to shine continuously, no matter his circumstances. Joseph knew God had a plan for his life. He just didn't know when, or how, it would all take place.

Potiphar, the jailer, and Pharaoh all knew that there was something different about Joseph. That is how Christians, Christ followers, are supposed to be. People around us should be able to tell that there is something different. Jesus told us to be a light on a hill.

{Turn on the flashlight. Ask:}

- If there is a light on a hill, can you hide it? [*Not easily*]

If we have Jesus as our Savior, then His light is inside of us, wanting to shine in everything we say and do.

{Ask:}

- How can you make your light shine? [*Allow answers; answers should include the idea of good works reflecting Jesus.*]

The first thing you must do is make sure that Jesus is your Savior. You can do good works and still be dead in sin. Once you are alive in Christ, then your works are different.

{Ask:}

- Do you think Joseph worked for Potiphar or for God? [*God*]
- Do you think Joseph worked for the jailer or for God? [*God*]
- Do you think Joseph worked for Pharaoh or for God? [*God*]

Joseph worked for God...and the Bible tells us that God was with Joseph and allowed him to succeed.

{Ask:}

- For whom should we work? [*God*]

When we decide to have Jesus as our Master and do works for Him, then we are a light to whoever is around us.

Like Joseph, we may have to make tough and sacrificial decisions to obey the Lord. Like Joseph, we might go through dark times and might deal with being forgotten. However, we must always remember that God was with Joseph and He blessed Joseph. If we stick with God, He'll do the same for us. Because of Joseph's loyalty to the Lord, God used him mightily to bring about His promise.

One thing that is SO neat about Joseph is that he KNEW God's promise would happen. Joseph knew that God would make a great nation of Abraham's family. Before he died, Joseph told his family to take his body with them when they left Egypt to occupy the land that God had promised. Remember, they were now living in Egypt, so mummification would allow this.

It was 400 years before Joseph's body was taken back to the land of Abraham, but God works in His time to do amazing things!

What can we learn from Joseph? If we decide to live the way God wants us to live, then we will be a light that shines in the darkness. It will not matter the circumstances we find ourselves in.

COMMENT BOX

■ ■

THINK: What went well as you taught this lesson? What can you do better?

_____

_____

_____

_____

_____

_____

_____

_____

_____

TIP: Discuss typical daily examples of behavior. Have the children decide if the flashlight should be turned off or on for each.

11

THE TEN PLAGUES

■ ■

The people of a nation are affected by the heart condition of their leader. This object lesson helps children describe why God sent the plagues and how they affected the Egyptians and the Hebrew people.

Scripture Focus: Exodus 7-11

Video: How I use the objects, and my thoughts on this lesson (see **Resources Page**)

Materials:

- Ancient Egypt TOOB (not necessary, but fun)
- Print PDF of Egyptian gods and goddesses (see **Resources Page**)
- Exodus 6:6 poster

Geography: Canaan, Egypt, and Goshen

"So tell the people of Israel that I say to them, 'I am the Lord. I will save you from the hard work the Egyptians force you to do. I will make you free. You will not be slaves to the Egyptians. I will free you by my great power. And I will punish the Egyptians terribly.' "

—Exodus 6:6 (ICB)

Background: Abraham passed the four-part covenant on to Isaac, who passed it on to Jacob. Jacob's name was changed to Israel. Jacob was the father of 12 sons. At his death, Israel passed on the promise to Judah, which is interesting because Judah is NOT the oldest son. In fact, he is fourth in line. Evidently the choices that Reuben, Simeon, and Levi made in Genesis 34-35:22 and 49:3-7 caused God to skip them and give the promise to Judah and his generations. Joseph had his roughly 70-member family living in the beautiful land of Goshen, which was THE prized land of Egypt. However, pharaohs come and go, and soon there were leaders who did not know Joseph.

OBJECT LESSON

■ ■

{Introduce ancient Egyptian history, either by having the children identify the contents of the TOOB, or by showing them the different gods and goddesses of Egypt. Even if you have the TOOB, you will want the images of the gods and goddesses for when we discuss the ten plagues.}

{Ask:}

- Do you know what these things are? [*Allow for answers to measure their knowledge of Egypt.*]

- Did Egyptians worship the One True God? [*No, they worshiped gods and goddesses that represented many different experiences of life.*]

In 400 years, the small family of Israel had grown to be between 2-3 million people. A pharaoh was on the throne who did not know Joseph. All he knew was that there was a HUGE number of people who were not Egyptians living in his country, and that they could take over the nation of Egypt if they so desired.

Therefore, the pharaoh enslaved every Hebrew. (The Israelites were also known as Hebrews because of the language they spoke.)

{Ask:}

- What is slavery? [*Slavery is when a group of people owns another group of people. The owned people are considered property and not as people.*]

The pharaoh decided that the number of Hebrews was growing too rapidly, so he had all the baby boys killed at birth.

A woman named Jochebed made an ark (or a basket) for her baby and placed it in the Nile River. The princess found the baby, allowed Jochebed to wean the child, and then brought him to the palace to live. Moses grew up in Pharaoh's house. He probably knew he was a Hebrew.

One day Moses watched an Egyptian beat a Hebrew slave. Moses killed the Egyptian and hid the body in the sand. He fled Egypt, knowing he would be sought after and killed. Moses fled to Midian where he married, had a family, and took care of sheep. God called Moses through the burning bush and sent Moses to meet his brother, Aaron. Then Moses was to get the children of Israel out of Egypt.

What is about to happen is the history of the destruction of one nation and the birth of another. God told Moses that Pharaoh's heart was hard. He also told Moses that He was going to bring judgments upon Egypt to bring out His people of Israel.

{As you go through the plagues, show the god or goddess who was rendered powerless. Be sure to emphasize what the people would have seen, smelled, heard, tasted, and touched.}

 ALL WATER TURNED TO BLOOD Khnum was the Egyptian god of creation and water. God destroyed the water by turning it to blood. The Egyptians went seven days searching for clean water to drink. All the fish died and the river stank. Pharaoh's magicians could do this "trick."

Pharaoh did not let the people go.

 FROGS Hequet was the goddess of fertility. The Egyptians believed she was the one who allowed babies to be created and born. She was represented by frogs. God had frogs come out of the Nile and go everywhere—in homes, ovens, and beds. The magicians could do this "trick" as well. The frogs died and were piled up in the streets. The land stank.

Pharaoh said the people could go...then he changed his mind.

 LICE Isis was the goddess of nature and magic. Thoth was the god of knowledge, wisdom, and magic. When God sent the plague of lice, the magicians knew they did not have the same power. They told Pharaoh, *"This was the finger of God."* Lice were on people and all beasts.

Pharaoh did not let the people go.

 FLIES Osiris was the god of life, death, resurrection, and sprouting vegetation. The swarms of flies from God destroyed plants and crops. The land of Goshen was set apart and did not experience the next five plagues.

Pharaoh said the people could go...then he changed his mind.

DEAD LIVESTOCK Apis was a god who looked like a bull. He was the god of strength and fertility. God had all the Egyptian cattle, horses, camels, donkeys, and sheep become diseased and die.

Pharaoh did not let the people go.

BOILS Serket was the goddess of medicine and magic. Moses and Aaron took ashes and scattered them toward heaven. Then God created boils and sores which broke out on man and whatever beasts were left. The magicians were unable to stand before Moses because of the boils. They were unable to help themselves.

Pharaoh did not let the people go.

THUNDER, HAIL, AND FIRE FROM HEAVEN Renenutet was the Egyptian goddess of nourishment and harvest. Moses warned Pharaoh to bring in the servants and whatever animals were left from the field. Those Egyptians who now feared God obeyed. Others did not. When God rained hail down, men, beasts, and all trees and plants were destroyed. There were no plants for nourishment and no harvest.

Pharaoh told Moses that he had *"sinned this time."* Pharaoh said the people could go...then he changed his mind.

LOCUSTS Bastet is the Egyptian goddess of protection. God sent the locusts. The locusts ate what was left after the hail, and they filled the homes of the Egyptians. Locusts covered the face of the earth. There was no protection. The people begged Pharaoh to let the Hebrews go. Did he not realize that "Egypt was destroyed"?

Pharaoh told Moses that he had *"sinned"* and asked for forgiveness. Pharaoh said the people could go...then he changed his mind.

DARKNESS Ra was the "main" god who was the god of the sun. God caused darkness to cover Egypt, but not the land of Goshen. For three days no one could see another, nor did the people move around.

Pharaoh told Moses he could take the people, but he had to leave the herds and flocks. But that would not do.

None of these "gods" could do anything. They were crafted by men and had no power. Only the One True God is living and all-powerful!

DEATH OF FIRSTBORN Anubis was the god of the afterlife who "weighed the heart" to see if a soul could enter the land of the dead. For this plague, God had the Hebrew people DO something to make sure they were safe. God commanded them to paint their doorposts with lambs' blood so God would not kill their firstborn. They had to obey, or death would enter their homes. However, the firstborn child of every Egyptian, from Pharaoh down to the prisoners, all died. There was a great cry throughout the land.

Pharaoh told Moses to take the people and be gone. The Egyptians urged the Hebrews to leave and gave them anything they wanted: clothes, riches, anything they asked. The Hebrews plundered, or took whatever they wanted, from the Egyptians.

LIFE APPLICATION

All throughout these verses of Scripture we hear about Pharaoh "hardening his heart." Eventually the Bible tells us that God hardened Pharaoh's heart. Scripture does not give us details about what this means, but what it does tell us is that God is concerned about our heart condition.

Does your heart belong to God? Or does it belong to you? Or does it belong to something else? God is jealous FOR you. He wants to bless you. He wants to forgive you. He wants to turn you into a better person. He wants to help you make good decisions. He wants to protect you. He wants to give you good health. He wants to be the One you go to when you have troubles. He wants to change your heart so that you can be like Jesus.

God knows your heart. He knows your thoughts. He knows you mess up. He knows your emotions. God loves you even when you sin. He also knows when you truly forgive someone. He knows if you truly love Him.

God knows your heart. Because He knows that you are a sinner, He sent Jesus to die for you so your heart could be without sin. You can be righteous, but Jesus has to do the work. You must believe that Jesus died on the cross, that He rose alive from the grave, and that He will return.

God knows if you really belong to Him. If you do, then eternal life is yours!

What can we learn from the ten plagues? God is all-powerful; man-made gods are not. He loves us and wants us to choose Him.

COMMENT BOX

████████████████████████████████

THINK: What went well as you taught this lesson? What can you do better?

_____

_____

_____

_____

_____

_____

_____

_____

_____

TIP: This is a large amount of Scripture, but to get the full effect, it is good to look at the whole plague event. Depending upon your time limit, you might want to do this lesson as two sessions.

12 THE PASSOVER

■ ■

Why is Jesus sometimes called the Passover Lamb? This Passover object lesson will explore the main events of this horrific incident in history when one nation is destroyed while another is born.

Scripture Focus: Exodus 11-12

Materials:

- Exodus 12:21 poster

Geography: Canaan, Egypt, and Goshen

Then Moses called all the elders of Israel together. He told them, "Get the animals for your families. Kill the animals for the Passover."

—Exodus 12:21 (ICB)

FUTUREFLYINGSAUCERS.COM

Background: Joseph had set his family of about 70 people up in the beautiful land of Goshen, which was THE prized land of Egypt. However, pharaohs came and went, and then there were leaders who did not know Joseph. The Israelites were forced into slavery, and God raised up Moses to be the deliverer. Pharaoh's heart had been hardened, even after nine horrible nationwide plagues that destroyed Egypt's economy and way of life. Pharaoh's heart still would not allow the people of Israel to leave his nation.

OBJECT LESSON

■ ■

{Split the children into two groups. Designate one group as the Egyptians and the other as the Hebrews.}

Nine plagues have taken place. The last one was darkness. All the land, except Goshen, had been plunged into darkness. Pharaoh, once again, would not allow the Hebrew people to leave.

{Ask the Egyptians:}

• What do you think about these plagues? [*Allow answers and discussion.*]

{Ask the Hebrews:}

• What do you think about these plagues? [*Allow answers and discussion.*]

{Use this as a time to review the other plagues, discuss the One True God versus the gods and goddesses of Egypt, and discuss slavery versus freedom.}

God told Moses about the final plague. Then Moses went to the Hebrews. He told them about the coming plague and what God wanted them to do.

Moses told Pharaoh that the firstborn sons of all Egypt, including the livestock (if any was still alive), would die.

{Tell the Egyptians to listen to what the Israelites had to do. As you describe the event, have the Hebrews act out these situations: pet the small lamb, kill the lamb, paint the door posts, cook, eat, pack clothes, put on shoes, hold a staff, and wait.}

The Hebrew families were told to take a one-year-old male lamb, or goat, without blemish and bring it into their homes. The lambs lived with each family for four days. Then the lamb was sacrificed, or killed.

The blood was painted on the outside of each family's door, on each doorpost and across the lentil.

The Hebrew families cooked and ate the lamb. They were to be prepared to leave at any moment. They had their shoes on and their staffs ready.

At the chosen time, midnight, God would pass through the land and kill the firstborn of man and beast. However, if God saw the blood on the doorway, He would then pass over that house.

{Have the Egyptians pretend to sleep sitting up. Then have those children who are firstborn to slump to the ground.}

The time came...and there was a great cry in Egypt. No family was spared. Pharaoh, who lost his own firstborn, told Moses and Aaron to take the people and leave.

{Have the Egyptians who are still "alive" to pretend to give the Israelites wealth and clothes.}

The Egyptian people gave the Hebrews silver, gold, and fine clothes. The riches of Egypt were taken out of the land of Egypt, as were the bones of Joseph.

LIFE APPLICATION

■ ■

{Ask:}

- What would the Hebrew people have smelled and tasted while waiting? [*Food, lamb, cooking*]

- What would the Egyptian people have seen when they woke up? [*A dead family member*]

- What did the Israelites hear as midnight faded to sunrise? [*The screams of the Egyptians*]

- What emotions do you think the Egyptians felt? [*Allow for answers.*]

- What emotions do you think the Israelites felt, especially when they realized they were free to go? [*Allow for answers.*]

This is such a heart-wrenching and tragic piece of history. The strong nation of Egypt was the ruling power of the world at this time. It was brought to ruin by the God of the universe supplying His own people with what they would need to begin their own nation. The economy was gone, agriculture was destroyed, people were dead, buildings and cities were probably damaged, and the armies of Pharaoh would be demolished at the Red Sea. What a picture of the power of God!

{Ask:}

- But don't forget about the blood! Who is God's firstborn Son? [*Jesus*]

- Moses delivered the Israelites. Who delivers us from our sins? [*Jesus*]

- Who saves every household from death? [*Jesus*]

- Whose blood do we need to paint on our hearts? [*Jesus'*]

- Who takes the consequences of God's wrath instead of us? [*Jesus*]

Jesus is the only One who can give salvation to us. We must be willing to accept and believe that Jesus died for us. We must be willing to confess with our mouths that Jesus is Lord and say that God raised Jesus from the dead...then we will be saved.

What can we learn from the Passover? Just as the Hebrew people were saved by the blood on the door, we can be saved by the blood of Christ.

COMMENT BOX

█ █

THINK: What went well as you taught this lesson? What can you do better?

_____

_____

_____

_____

_____

_____

_____

_____

_____

TIP: The Passover is another picture God is giving to us that depicts Jesus' death. Life comes from the blood. Thank God now for covering you in the blood of Christ.

13 MOSES AND THE LAW

■ ■

With a satellite navigation system, it can be difficult to get lost. However, relying on technology that could be incorrect might steer you in the wrong direction. This object lesson teaches children the purpose of the Law and what Jesus expects from those who follow Him.

Scripture Focus: Exodus 20

Materials:

- Road map (paper, not digital)
- Exodus 20:2 poster

Geography: Egypt, Israel, and the Red Sea

"I am the Lord your God. I brought you out of the land of Egypt where you were slaves. You must not have any other gods except me."

—Exodus 20:2-3 (ICB)

FUTUREFLYINGSAUCERS.COM

Background: The Israelites were forced into slavery, and God raised up Moses to be their deliverer. Pharaoh's heart had been hardened. Even after nine horrible nationwide plagues that destroyed Egypt's economy and way of life, Pharaoh still would not allow the people of Israel to leave his nation. The tenth and final plague caused a cry to be heard throughout Egypt as God killed the firstborn of all Egypt, passing over the homes with the blood of the lamb on the doors.

OBJECT LESSON

{Show the map. Unfold it or show the pages if it's a book.}

The reason we use maps is so we can find our way. To get where we are going, we have to follow the rules. We have to drive the speed limit. We can't drive down the median. We stop at traffic lights and obey traffic signs.

{Ask:}

- Why is it important to follow driving rules? [*They keep us safe and allow us to reach our destination.*]

- What happens if I don't follow the rules of the state when I am driving? [*You will get pulled over by the police and get a ticket.*]

- What happens if I do not follow the directions when I drive somewhere? [*You will not reach the place you desire to go.*]

{Tell a quick story about a time when you were driving and did not follow the rules, or a time when you got lost.}

BIBLE LESSON

■ ■

As the Hebrews left Egypt, they carried along with them riches given to them by the Egyptian people. Moses, directed by God, had the people follow an angel of the Lord in the form of a pillar of cloud by day and a pillar of fire by night. (A pillar is a column.)

Pharaoh allowed the people to leave and then changed his mind once again. He and the army of Egypt went in pursuit. The Israelites panicked because they had reached the Red Sea with no way across. Moses told them, *"The Lord will fight for you!"*

Moses obeyed God and raised his staff. The water divided, and the Hebrew people crossed over on dry land. The Egyptians tried to cross as well, but God thwarted their way and caused the wheels to fall off their chariots. Once the Hebrew people were on the other side, the waters crashed down and the army of Egypt disappeared.

The Israelites walked on. Soon they began to complain to Moses. They said they had no water or food. They said that they should return to Egypt. In each situation, the Lord provided for the Israelites' needs. He provided water from rocks, quail for meat, and bread from heaven. The people traveled for three months until they reached Mt. Sinai.

God gave the Israelites some rules called the Ten Commandments. These commandments would be the Law that everyone in the nation would follow. These laws were given to the people by God to protect them, to set them apart from the other nations, and to teach them how to live for God.

{Ask:}

- Do you have rules in your home? [*Yes*]
- What are some of the rules in your family home? [*Allow answers.*]
- Why do your parents want you to follow those rules? [*Allow answers, including to get along with family members, to keep us safe, etc.*]
- Does your school have rules? [*Yes*]
- Does our nation have rules? [*Yes*]

- What happens if you decide to not follow the rules in your home? [*Consequence*]

- What happens if you decide to not follow the rules of our nation? [*Go to court before a judge, be fined or go to prison*]

- What happens if you decide to not follow God's rules? [*Allow for answers; the children might say similar answers as above. They might be confused because God won't physically put someone in jail or give a consequence. Lead the kids to see that consequences still happen when we disobey God, but it might not happen immediately.*]

- If you choose to go against God's rules will you have a good relationship with Him? [*No*]

The first four laws deal with the people's relationship with God. The last six deal with the people's relationships with each other.

God was setting up His nation. He had many people who needed leadership and organization as they traveled and as they entered the land.

God knew what obstacles the people would be facing. He wanted to protect His nation. The Law was not set up to make the Israelites miserable, but to help them be a people who reflected the nature of God to the world.

LIFE APPLICATION

■ ■

{Ask:}

• Was there any way the Israelites could keep the whole Law perfectly? [*No*]

In fact, the Bible tells us that even if you keep ALL the commandments and break just one, that you have broken all of them. We are sinners. We are not perfect. The Law tells us what we cannot do. And because we cannot keep the Law of God, we deserve death.

{Ask:}

• Who is the only One who has followed the whole Law? [*Jesus*]

Jesus chose to take your place in death because He can follow the entire Law without messing up. He took your punishment. What a great gift! He did it because He loves you.

Jesus was asked, *"What is the greatest commandment?"*

His answer was this: *"Love the Lord your God with all your heart, with all your soul, and with all your mind. And the second is like it—love your neighbor as yourself"* (Matthew 22:36-40).

Those two commands wrap up all the other ten: Love God and then love people.

Jesus tells us in John 15:10 that those who abide with Him follow His commands. Abiding, dwelling, living a life with Jesus—this goes together with obeying God's commands. If you want to abide, then you must be obeying. If you are not obeying God's commands, then you do not have a good relationship with Jesus and you are not abiding in Jesus.

God is not trying to make your life miserable. He desires to protect you from environments or decisions that could harm you. For example, if you decided to break God's rule for stealing, you could end up in jail for a long time. That would mess up your life and your relationships with people. That's not good. God wants to bless you. Most of the time He blesses when you choose to obey Him.

What can we learn from Moses and the Ten Commandments? The purpose of the Law is to show us our sin and why we need Jesus. By abiding in Jesus and obeying the best we can, we can have a healthy and fulfilling life that glorifies God.

COMMENT BOX

THINK: What went well as you taught this lesson? What can you do better?

_____

_____

_____

_____

_____

_____

_____

_____

_____

TIP: See the Resources Page for a fun extra lesson that uses hand motions to memorize the Ten Commandments.

14 THE TWELVE SPIES AND THE WANDERING

■■■■■■■■■■■■■■■■■■■■■■■■■

We like to exaggerate situations at times. We claim we cannot do something because the task seems huge and daunting. This object lesson about the 12 spies will help our children understand that with Jesus we have already won the victory, even if life seems hard.

Scripture Focus: Numbers 13

Materials:

- Toy plastic insects
- Numbers 13:30 poster

Geography: Kadesh (Paran) and Canaan

Background: The Israelites were given freedom from Egypt by the miraculous hand of God. God gave the Israelites some rules called the Ten Commandments. These commandments would be the Law that everyone in the nation should follow. These laws were given to the people by God to protect them, to set them apart from the other nations, and to teach them how to live for God.

Then Caleb told the people near Moses to be quiet. Caleb said, "We should go up and take the land for ourselves. We can do it."

—Numbers 13:30 (ICB)

FUTUREFLYINGSAUCERS.COM

By the time the Hebrews reached Mt. Sinai, they had seen many wonders by God. They were beginning to see God fulfill His promises to Abraham. A nation was beginning to form. A great nation needs rules and they now had the Ten Commandments, as well as many other laws and regulations. God had given Moses the directions to build the Tabernacle, and the priesthood was set up through the tribe of Levi and the family of Aaron.

OBJECT LESSON

■ ■

{Choose four or five of the insects. Be sure one is a grasshopper. Hold up each one and have the children identify the insects. Ask:}

- Are these toy insects big or small? [*Compared to the real insects, these are very big.*]

- If this grasshopper were real and it looked around the room, would it think it was big or small? [*Small*]

- How would the grasshopper perceive us in the room? [*It would think we were giants. Be sure to get the word "giants" from the kids.*]

- Since these pretend insects are bigger than real insects, can we say that they are "exaggerated"? Bigger than they really are? [*Yes*]

BIBLE LESSON

■ ■ ■ ■ ■ ■ ■ ■ ■ ■ ■ ■ ■ ■ ■ ■ ■ ■ ■ ■

{The following chart is a mnemonic to help remember the names of the 12 tribes. Challenge the kids to memorize the 12 names.}

TWELVE TRIBES OF ISRAEL												
S.	J.	B	E	D	M	I	Z	A	N,	M	G	R.
I	U	E	P	A	A	S	E	S	A	A	A	E
M	D	N	H	N	N	S	B	H	P	N	D	U
E	A	J	R		A	A	U	E	H	A		B
O	H	A	A		S	C	L	R	T	S		E
N		M	I		S	H	U		A	S		N
		I	M		E	A	N		L	E		
		N			H	R			I	H		

{Ask:}

- Who can name the 12 tribes? [*They probably will not be able to.*]
- Who can name at least one of the sons of Jacob? [*Joseph, might name Reuben or Judah if they remember the story of Joseph being sold into slavery*]

When the Israelites were at Mt. Sinai, Moses needed to get the people organized. Remember, God is making a great nation. To have a great nation, there needs to be people. Those people need to be organized. God gave them laws, and Moses counted the people. He had all the people gather by families, or tribes. Each tribe was named after one of the sons of Jacob.

S. J. BEDMIZAN is going to help us to remember the 12 tribes. Because the people needed to be organized, or managed, S. J. BEDMIZAN is a manager, or MGR.

{Read through all the names of the tribes. Ask:}

- What do you notice about these names? Are these all the names? [*There is no tribe of Joseph. There is also no tribe of Levi shown. Manasseh is listed two times.*]

All the people of Israel were organized by tribe. Remember, Jacob had 12 sons. One of those sons, Levi, would be given the responsibility of the Tabernacle and be given certain cities within each tribe.

There is no tribe of Joseph. When Jacob was dying, he blessed each of his sons. Joseph received a double portion of the blessing and so his sons, Ephraim and Manasseh, are listed as two separate tribes. When the tribes eventually settled in the Promised Land, Manasseh received a double portion of land.

The tribes were organized, and the people traveled to Kadesh. God told Moses to send 12 spies into the Promised Land to scout it out. One spy was to come from each tribe. You know the spy Hoshea well. Moses changed his name to Joshua. Name changing is important! This shows us that God is going to do something amazing with Joshua. Another well-known spy is Caleb. He came from the tribe of Judah.

The spies were gone 40 days.

When they returned, the spies reported to the people that the land was just as God described. There was wonderful land! The fruit was magnificent! In fact, two men carried back a huge cluster of grapes!

Joshua and Caleb: *"Let's go take the land!"*

10 other spies: *"No! There are large cities and the people are GIANTS!"*

They recommended NOT going into the Promised Land. The other two spies, Joshua and Caleb, encouraged the people to go and take the land.

Joshua and Caleb: *"God is on our side! Let us go up at once! Do not rebel or fear! The Lord is with us!"*

10 spies and the people: *"No!"*

Caleb and Joshua tore their clothes in agony. The Israelites were in the process of picking up stones to hurl at Joshua and Caleb when a heavenly voice called out, and God's glory appeared in the tabernacle.

That voice condemned the Hebrew people for their disobedience. Because of their bad choice to not go into the land, the Hebrews would be required to wander in the desert for 40 years. All the Israelites would die, and their children would be the ones to receive the blessing of the Promised Land. All would die, except for two men: Caleb and Joshua.

LIFE APPLICATION

{Show the grasshopper.}

The 10 spies who led the rebellion against Moses, Joshua, and Caleb said that the Hebrew people were like grasshoppers compared to the giants of the land.

{Ask:}

- Do you think the ten spies were exaggerating? [*Yes*]

Sometimes when we face a hard situation we think we are too little, too unintelligent, or too untalented to do the job. We think we are grasshoppers compared to the "giants" we are facing. We exaggerate the situation and make it larger than it really is. We forget that God already won the victory.

Joshua and Caleb continued to encourage the Hebrew people and reminded them that God was on their side. Taking the land was going to be challenging work, but God was on their side. They could not lose!

But the people rebelled and disobeyed God. Consequently, they all died in the wilderness.

Obedience is a big deal to God. In Scripture, God tells us that if we love Him, then we will keep, or obey, His commandments. Disobedience is sin and will have consequences, just as the Hebrews received a consequence. On the other hand, obedience comes with rewards, although not necessarily rewards here on earth. God certainly does bless those who love and obey Him, but obedience means heavenly rewards.

The Bible tells us something wonderful about Caleb. It says that he had a different spirit in him and that he followed God fully. Isn't that what you want? If you have faith in Jesus, then you have a different spirit inside you, the Holy Spirit. And when we follow Jesus by obeying Him, then we follow Him fully.

What can we learn from the 12 spies and the wandering? We need to be like Joshua and Caleb who were ready to obey God even if the fight was going to be hard. We do not want to be like the other 10 spies who rebelled and encouraged others to disobey God as well.

COMMENT BOX

████████████████████████████████

THINK: What went well as you taught this lesson? What can you do better?

_____

_____

_____

_____

_____

_____

_____

_____

_____

TIP: This is a wonderful passage to dramatize with your voice. Talk as the 10 spies and then have Joshua and Caleb respond. Model the conversation, and then add in the response of the Israelites.

15 JOSHUA TAKES COMMAND

■ ■

FEAR. You cannot see it, but you can surely see the effects of it. In this object lesson, use a simple science experiment to help children understand that God asks us to make tough decisions and that He is with us wherever we go.

Scripture Focus: Joshua 1 and 5:13-15

Materials:

- Wide candle
- Lighter or matches
- Glass beaker or measuring cup
- White vinegar
- Baking soda
- See the **Resources Page** for a video showing you how to do this science experiment, and for a video showing the archeological excavation of the walls of Jericho and how they prove this event in the Bible to be true.
- Joshua 1:7 poster

Geography: Israel, Jordan River

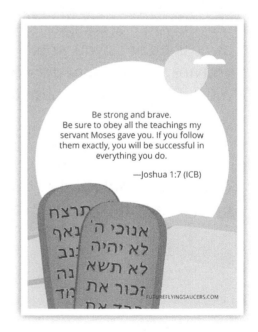

Be strong and brave.
Be sure to obey all the teachings my
servant Moses gave you. If you follow
them exactly, you will be successful in
everything you do.

—Joshua 1:7 (ICB)

Background: Because of their choice not to go into the land, the Hebrews would be required to wander the desert for 40 years. All the Israelites would die. Their children would be the ones to receive the blessing of the Promised Land. All would die, except for two men: Caleb and Joshua.

OBJECT LESSON

■ ■

{Put the candle, the lighter, and the other materials on a table in front of you. Light the candle. Ask:}

- Of which words of Jesus does this candle remind you? [*Allow for answers. Jesus is the Light of the World; lead children to the answer of us being a light on a hill.*]

Jesus told us to be a light on a hill. We are to shine for Him and show people the love of God in everything we do. Therefore, we shine, especially when life is good.

{Put some of the baking soda in the measuring cup and add some vinegar. Put your hand over the top as the chemical reaction takes place. Then "pour" the gas over the candle to put it out. It will seem as though something invisible put out the candle.}

When life gets hard, our light can go out. Maybe you get scared and fearful. Maybe you are comparing yourself to other people. Perhaps you aren't as good at basketball as you would like to be. Maybe your parents are fighting a lot, and you are scared about divorce. Maybe you have a tough time at school. Maybe you must do a report and have to stand in front of people.

You can't see the fear, but you feel it. And it can put out your light if you are not careful.

{Light the candle and go through the experiment again. Reinforce the concept of fear putting out their candles.}

BIBLE LESSON

■ ■

At the beginning of the book of Joshua, God told Joshua that Moses had died. God put Joshua in charge of all the people. This was a huge, hard task that was handed to Joshua.

The Lord told Joshua that wherever his foot went, that land would be given to the people. God again promised to give them the land which He promised Abraham.

Over and over, God told Joshua to be strong and courageous. God knew that taking the land was going to be hard. There were big cities, like Jericho. There were fierce people who lived in those cities. Joshua was going to be leading the people to do some hard things. He would need to be strong and courageous.

{Light the candle.}

Joshua was told that God would be with him. Then God told Joshua to be careful about something. God wanted Joshua to keep his light shining. Joshua was going to be a leader of a nation that was about to divide and conquer other nations. Therefore, he needed to be careful.

{Read through Joshua 1:7-9. Stop after each phrase or so, and ask a question to make sure the children understand what the Scripture means. You can be humorous about it, especially the verse about "keeping the law on our lips." Put your Bible by your mouth and ask if this is what the Scripture is saying to do.}

- What does "careful" mean? [*Allow for answers; doing something slowly; taking your time; focusing on something important*]
- How much of the law was Joshua to obey? [*All of it*]
- What does it mean to not turn to the right or the left? [*Allow for answers. Have the kids think about a horse and rider. The rider can turn the horse to the right or the left, but not if he wants it to walk straight. The law keeps us walking like Jesus. But if we stop obeying, we turn away to the right or the left, and we sin.*]

After God gave Joshua these directions, Joshua led the people across the Jordan River. Then they began the process of taking over the land of Canaan.

Before the battle of Jericho, Joshua received a visitor. The Commander of the Army of the Lord appeared to him. The commander had a sword and Joshua asked, *"Are you for us? or for our enemies?"*

"Neither, but as the Commander of the Lord's army, I come," replied the man.

Joshua fell to his face and asked what message the Lord had for him. The man proceeded to tell Joshua how to go about taking the city of Jericho. God was going to have the light of an entire nation shine throughout the darkness of that land.

LIFE APPLICATION

{Put the candle out with the invisible gas.}

Joshua faced many fears during the years it took to take over the land for the nation of Israel. And when the light did go out, when things went wrong, God told Joshua that there was sin in the camp.

{Ask:}

- When you sin, are you walking straight with Jesus? Or have you turned to the right or left away from Him? [*Turned away from Him*]
- How do we get back to walking straight with Jesus? [*By asking for forgiveness and obeying His commands*]

We can either serve and obey the Lord, or we can serve ourselves and do what we want. Conquering the land was challenging work. It involved sacrifice.

There are many things in life today that are hard to do. We would much rather watch TV than clean our rooms. We would rather ride bikes and not do homework. Watching TV and riding bikes are easy. God does not call His people to an easy life.

He asks us to do hard things. He asks us to choose the needs of others before our own. He asks us to be holy and pure as He is. He asks us to deny ourselves, pick up our cross, and follow Him. God wants us to be fishers of men.

Jesus did not want to die on the cross. In fact, He asked God if He really had to do it. But Jesus chose to do the hard thing. He knew we needed Him to die so we could have eternal life. Jesus gave up what He wanted in order to be obedient. And because of His obedience, we receive salvation.

{Light the candle.}

Jesus is the Light of the World. We are to be lights on top of a hill.

What can we learn from Joshua? We can be strong and courageous because God is with us wherever we go. We do not need to fear anything.

COMMENT BOX

■ ■

THINK: What went well as you taught this lesson? What can you do better?

_____

_____

_____

_____

_____

_____

_____

_____

_____

TIP: Be sure to practice this experiment a few times. It is tricky to capture the gas. It is really neat when the flame goes out.

16 JUDGES

■■■■■■■■■■■■■■■■■■■■■■■■■■

The cycle of sin—what is it and how do we deal with it? This object lesson from the Book of Judges explains the cycle of sin and compares the Israelites' cycle with our own.

Scripture Focus: Judges 2:7-23

Materials:

- Paper plate (see images for labeling both sides)
- Scissors
- 3-4 M.C. Escher pictures (I copied the image and then pasted it into a Word document. Because of copyright, I cannot give you those images. See the **Resources Page** for a link that takes you to the Escher Gallery.)
- Judges 2:10 poster

Geography: Israel

After those people had died, their children grew up. They did not know the Lord or what he had done for Israel.

—Judges 2:10 (ICB)

FUTUREFLYINGSAUCERS.COM

Background: Joshua and the Israelites took the Promised Land by entering westward over the Jordan River and then dividing the land in half. There was a southern campaign and then a northern campaign to conquer all the cities and peoples. Before he died, Joshua gave the nation a farewell address. He told the people to finish conquering the Canaanites and to remember everything that they had seen the Lord do for them. He encouraged them to be strong and to obey the Lord. Then he warned the people to get rid of the idols in the land. In conclusion, Joshua challenged the people to choose: *"Choose this day whom you will serve. As for me and my house we shall serve the Lord."*

OBJECT LESSON

■ ■

{Show each piece of art to the children. Have them describe what they see, and discuss how the images trick their eyes. These are fun pictures!}

M.C. Escher was a graphic artist who loved architecture and fantasy. Many of his artworks play with optical illusions and buildings. It is great fun to look at his drawings and see how they trick your eyes.

These fun pictures tricked our eyes. Our eyes can be tricked into seeing something that isn't true.

{Ask:}

- Have you ever thought or said something about a person only to find out later that you were wrong? [*Allow for answers.*]

There are going to be plenty of times in life when this happens. Our eyes and ears can deceive us.

BIBLE LESSON

■ ■

Israel was a theocracy, which means it was a nation that was led by God. God had used Moses to bring the people from Egypt, and He had used Joshua to take over the land of Canaan.

Joshua led the Hebrews for about 50 years. The tribes of Israel were comprised of people who had been born during the years of wandering. They had seen God's hand at work as they conquered the wicked people who lived in the land.

Once Joshua and the last of the elders from that generation had died, there was no leadership, no king, and no real government. God was to be the leader. However, following a faceless God is a hard thing to do, and each tribe did its own thing instead. They did not conquer the rest of the Canaanites as they were told to, even though God sent messages to them to be obedient. An entire generation grew up not knowing anything about God.

Therefore, God had the Canaanites stay in the land to test the faith of His people. And they failed miserably. The people fell into gross idolatry and gross immorality to the point that *everyone did what was right in their own eyes."*

{Ask:}

- What do we know about our eyes? [*They can deceive us.*]
- What might happen if we only trust our eyes? [*Bad things might happen. We might make poor choices.*]

The book of Judges spans about 400 years. During those years, there are many cycles of one certain behavior.

1. The people sinned against God by worshiping idols and living unholy lives.

2. God sent an oppressor/army/disaster to trouble Israel.

3. The people cried out to God for help and repented.

4. God showed pity and brought about deliverance through a judge.

5. The judge led the people until he died and then the people sinned again...etc.

There are certain phrases that are repeated in the book of Judges. One is *"everyone did what was right in their own eyes."* Another is *"and the children of Israel did evil in the sight of the Lord."*

The Hebrew people were to be led by God. Even when Moses was leading them, the people didn't want to interact with God much. They would listen to Moses and Joshua. They would obey at times. But once they were in the land on their own, the Israelites forgot God. Most parents did not teach their children about God like they were supposed to; therefore, most of the children grew up not knowing about Him. *"Everyone did what was right in their own eyes."* The people rejected God's ways.

LIFE APPLICATION

■ ■

{Show the paper plate for the book of Judges.}

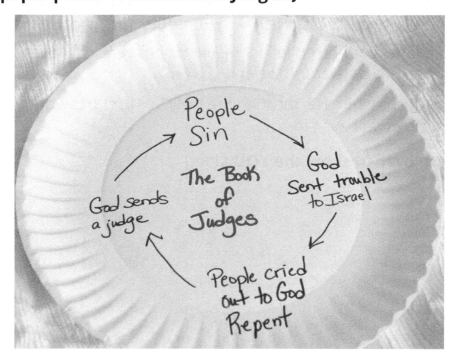

{Ask:}

- In the book of Judges, what was the first thing that happened in the cycle? [*The people did what was right in their own eyes and sinned against God.*]

- What happened next? [*God sent an army to trouble or oppress Israel.*]

- Then what happened? [*The people cried out to God and repented of their sin.*]

- What did God do in response? [*God found a judge that saved Israel from the enemy, and the judge was in charge until his/her death.*]

- What happened after the judge died? [*The people sinned again, even worse than before.*]

- Did you know YOU have a cycle like this? [*Allow for answers, but they might be surprised.*]

The Israelites were supposed to follow a faceless God. But the faceless God decided to send His Son to the earth. NOW God had a face! Jesus told His followers, "*When you see Me, you see the Father.*"

We have the letters of the New Testament that tell us all about Jesus, what He did, and how He treated people. We know that He lived and died and rose again.

{Ask:}

- Have you ever seen Jesus? [*No*]

- How do we know that He is real? [*The people of the Bible physically encountered Him. They are witnesses. They lived with Him. They saw what He did.*]

- Have you ever encountered Jesus? [*Allow for answers. Only those who have been saved can honestly answer this well.*]

You encounter Jesus when He, through the Holy Spirit, starts working in your heart. You start realizing you have sin.

{Flip the plate over to show the YOU side.}

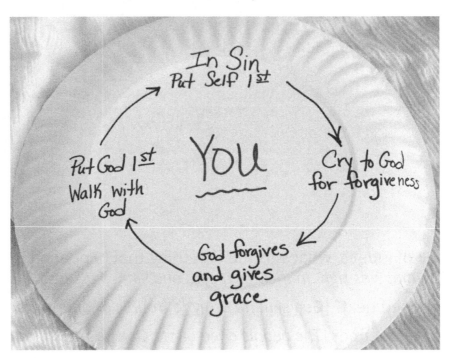

You have a cycle like the Israelites.

1. You are born into sin when you are born.

2. At some point, you realize that you don't please God with some of the things you think, say, and do. When you realize this, you go to God.

3. You go to Jesus and you ask Him to forgive you. You tell Him that you are sorry and that you want to live HIS way and not YOUR way.

4. God responds by forgiving, giving you grace and mercy. The Holy Spirit begins to live inside of you.

5. Then you walk with God. You read your Bible. You are nice to people. You do good things. You are putting God first.

6. Then you sin and put yourself first again.

And so on and so on.

Your cycle of sin and forgiveness can be different from the Israelites ONLY if Jesus is your Savior. **Instead of seeing life through your own eyes, you see life through the eyes of Jesus.**

{With the scissors, cut the plate into a spiral.}

Some people choose to stay in their sin. They encounter Jesus and reject Him just like the Israelites did. Maybe that's where you are right now. Do you know you are a sinner? Is God working in your heart?

When a person chooses to believe in Jesus and live God's way, then this new cycle begins.

{Stretch out the spiral.}

Our goal is to be more and more like Jesus. Every time we sin, and we go to God for forgiveness, and He gives us grace, and we walk with Him...every time this cycle happens, God changes us to be more and more like Jesus.

{Point to the top of the spiral.}

We will never reach the goal of behaving like Jesus until we are in heaven with Him. However, every day we can get a little bit closer to the goal.

{Ask:}

- Do you go to God when you have sinned? [*Allow for answers.*]
- Do you ask for forgiveness and repent? [*Allow for answers.*]

What can we learn from the book of Judges? All people live in a cycle of sin and rebellion. It is only through Jesus that we can break the cycle and have a new cycle that changes us into the image of Jesus.

COMMENT BOX

███ █ █ █ █ █ █ █ █ █ █ █ █ █ █ █ ██

THINK: What went well as you taught this lesson? What can you do better?

_____

_____

_____

_____

_____

_____

_____

_____

_____

TIP: Where are you on the sin and forgiveness cycle right now? Talk to the Lord. Make sure you are right with Him, and be encouraged.

17

SAMUEL, THE ARK, AND THE PHILISTINES

■■■■■■■■■■■■■■■■■■■■■■■■■■■■

Do you ever blow the dice while playing a game? Does your favorite team rub a rock before charging down a hill to play football? What habits of "luckiness" exist around you? In this object lesson about Samuel, the Ark, and the Philistines, children will learn that God is not a good luck charm and that blessings come from obedience.

Focus Scripture: 1 Samuel 3-6

Materials:

- A "lucky" item, like a rabbit's foot or a ball cap
- Map (see **Resources Page**)
- 1 Samuel 3:10 poster

Geography: Shiloh, Ebenezer, Ashdod, Gath, Ekron, Beth Shemesh

Background: During the years of the judges, there was great sin and darkness. After Joshua died, there was no leadership, no king, and no government. Each tribe ruled itself. The people fell into gross idolatry and gross immorality to the point that *"everyone did what was right in their own eyes."* HOWEVER God did not forget His promise to Abraham. He was at work through a young Moabite lady named Ruth. Through Ruth, God would bring about a king and THE King.

The Lord came and stood there. He called as he had before. He said, "Samuel, Samuel!" Samuel said, "Speak, Lord. I am your servant, and I am listening."

—1 Samuel 3:10 (ICB)

FUTUREFLYINGSAUCERS.COM

The Israelites had the Tabernacle where the priests and Levites ministered to God. But even there, God's voice was silent because of the amount of sin in the land.

OBJECT LESSON

■ ■

{Hold up the "lucky" item. I used a baseball cap and told the kids it was my "lucky Bible teaching hat." It was quite funny because I proceeded to tell the story and got all the numbers wrong! (Accidentally!) The kids thought it was great and that my hat did not help at all! Ask:}

- If I take this item to a ballgame, that means my team will win, right? [*Allow for answers.*]

- If I forget to take it, then my team will lose. Is this right? [*Allow for answers.*]

- Why do people throw coins into a water fountain? [*Allow for answers.*]

- During St. Patrick's Day, what is the object that supposedly will bring you good luck? [*Four-leaf clover*]

- What IS "good luck"? [*Allow for answers.*]

- Can objects bring about good luck? [*Allow for answers.*]

Many people enjoy having "lucky" items, or things that they think might bring them good luck. People want to win ball games. They want situations to turn out with good results.

{Ask:}

- If you use a certain baseball bat and then you get many hits during a game or season using that bat, is it really the BAT that allowed you to be successful? [*Allow for answers.*]

- What is the Ark of the Covenant? [*When the Israelites received the directions from God through Moses to build the Tabernacle, there were also directions on what to put IN the tabernacle: furniture, candles, curtains, etc. The Ark of the Covenant was to be built as the place where God would sit—the Mercy Seat. There were very specific rules as to who could carry the Ark and how it was to be moved. The priests knew if anyone touched the Ark, he would be killed. The Ark was placed in the Holy of Holies, and only the high priest was to enter the room once per year.*]

- What is a prophecy? [*A prediction about a future event; usually calls for people to repent*]

- What is a prophet? [*A person who receives prophecies from God; a person who prays to God in order to save/spare the lives of others*]

BIBLE LESSON

{As you tell the events, have the map nearby so you can follow the Ark as it moves.}

During the time of the Judges, a father and mother had a baby. That baby was Samuel. Samuel was raised in the Tabernacle and served the Lord.

When Samuel was a boy, *"The word of the Lord was rare."* In fact, when Samuel heard the Lord's voice, he thought it was Eli.

Samuel heard a voice say, *"Samuel! Samuel!"* After three times of going to Eli to ask what he wanted, Eli told Samuel that it must be the Lord speaking to him. Eli told Samuel to tell the voice, *"Speak, for your servant hears."*

The next time Samuel heard the voice, he responded, and Samuel received his first prophecy from the Lord. God told Samuel that He was going to take the priesthood away from the family of Eli because of the evil doings of Eli's sons. The next morning Eli asked Samuel about God's words. Samuel told him.

Israel and the Philistines went to war at Ebenezer. Israel lost about 4,000 men and wondered why they had been defeated. They went into the Tabernacle and some priests (Hophni and Phinehas, Eli's sons) brought the Ark of the Covenant out of the Holy of Holies so they could take it to battle with them.

The army of Israel took the Ark of the Covenant into battle hoping they would win. They thought God was a good luck charm. It did not work. In fact, not only did the army lose 30,000 men, but the Ark of the Covenant was captured by the enemy! During the battle Eli's two sons were killed. When Eli heard that his sons had been killed and the Ark had been captured, he fell backward, broke his neck, and died. Therefore, the prophecy of Samuel came true.

{Follow the Ark as it travels.}

The Philistines took the Ark to the town of **Ashdod**. They put it in the temple of a grain god called Dagon. They went to bed. In the morning, the statue of Dagon was on its face in front of the Ark. The people righted the statue. The next morning, the statue was on its face again and the hands and head had been broken off. The Lord was against the people and they developed diseases and had tumors grow on them.

The Ark was moved to **Gath**. The people there were struck with destruction and tumors, too. Then they sent the ark to **Ekron**. The people there wanted nothing to do with the Ark, so they decided to send it back to Israel.

They built a new wagon, yoked two mother cows to it, put the Ark on the cart, and sent it down the road. It traveled to **Beth-Shemesh**, which was a Levite town. The people there did not know how to treat the Ark, and some of the men looked into it and died. They passed the Ark on to **Kiriath-jearim,** where it stayed for 20 years.

At the end of the 20 years, Samuel was grown up and told the people to meet him at Mizpah. They did. He told them that they had been sinning against God and needed to repent. The people did, and while they were sacrificing to God, the Philistines decided to attack. The Israelites attacked, fought back, and WON.

No good luck charm was needed.

LIFE APPLICATION

■ ■

God is not someone to trifle with. He takes sin seriously. The Hebrew people were being defeated because they were disobedient to God. He allowed them to have consequences for their actions.

If everyone was doing what was right in their own eyes, then why should God help them?

Relationships are formed between two persons. Our relationship with God is between us and God—between you and Him. If we listen to God as Samuel did, then God will speak and bless. If we only consider God on our terms, then He's not going to work "magic" for us.

The Israelites were strong against the Philistines the second time because their relationship with God was strong again. This does not mean that if we are close to God, nothing bad will happen to us. The Philistines STILL attacked. The difference was that God was with His people and gave them strength to stand up to the enemy.

What can we learn from Samuel and the Israelites? Good luck charms are not what we need. We need God to help us in everything!

COMMENT BOX

■ ■

THINK: What went well as you taught this lesson? What can you do better?

_____

_____

_____

_____

_____

_____

_____

_____

_____

TIP: To hear God, we need to pray. For a practical way to teach children to pray, see the Resources Page.

18 ANOINTING KING DAVID

■■■■■■■■■■■■■■■■■■■■■■■■■■■■■

Many children think that if they act good on the outside, then it does not matter what is going on in their hearts on the inside. God cares about the heart. In this object lesson, children will learn that God sees their hearts and that they must decide what they want Him to see.

Scripture Focus: 1 Samuel 16:1-13

Materials:

- Candy box filled with yucky treats (onions, stinky socks, banana peels...)
- Clear, empty candy or cookie jar
- Fruit-shaped candy (put the candy in the glass jar)
- 1 Samuel 16:7 poster

{I bought a Whitman's Sampler for the box and Heller and Strauss Tutti Frutti candies for the fruit-shaped candy and glass jar. I spent more money on this object lesson than I normally do, but when I found the candy jar, I could not resist! It worked perfectly!}

But the Lord said to Samuel, "Don't look at how handsome Eliab is. Don't look at how tall he is. I have not chosen him. God does not see the same way people see. People look at the outside of a person, but the Lord looks at the heart."

—1 Samuel 16:7 (ICB)

Geography: Israel, David's kingdom

Background: The people of Israel told Samuel that they wanted a king so they could be like "all of the other nations." Saul, who was literally a head taller than everyone else, was chosen. He had the opportunity to lead the people of God and help Israel become a great nation. Instead, he would have the kingdom ripped from his grasp. He made selfish, disobedient decisions, and Samuel told Saul that God had rejected him as king.

OBJECT LESSON

■ ■

{Show the closed box with the yucky stuff hidden. Keep the clear jar hidden. Ask:}

- What is this? [*Allow for answers.*]

- What comes inside a box like this? [*Yummy candy*]

- What is your favorite kind of candy from boxes like this? [*Allow for answers. Be sure to discuss the diverse types of candy and react in a way that shows you LOVE eating this candy.*]

This box looks brand new. I bet the candy is brand new. Let's open the box!

{Show the stinky, yucky stuff and make an awful face when you smell the trash. Ask:}

- Ugh! What is this? [*Allow for answers.*]

- But the box looked SO nice and new! Are you surprised by what we found inside? [*Allow for answers.*]

- Can you always trust that you will find the correct thing inside a labeled box? [*Most of the time, but not this time!*]

Everything about the outside of the box told me the inside should be good...but it was not.

BIBLE LESSON

■ ■

Saul knew that God would take the kingdom away from him eventually. Saul became suspicious and unruly. The Scriptures say that the Spirit of the Lord left Saul, and there were times when God allowed an evil spirit to enter Saul.

God sent Samuel to anoint the new king. Fearing King Saul, Samuel asked God how he could get away with anointing another king while Saul was still alive and could catch him. God gave specific instructions to Samuel that would cover and protect his reason for going to Bethlehem. Samuel followed God's directions and took a heifer, a female cow, with him to Bethlehem to sacrifice there.

He asked a man named Jessie, of Bethlehem, in the tribe of Judah, to sacrifice with him. (Jessie's grandmother was Ruth!) Samuel began to look through all of Jessie's sons. *"Surely THIS is the one, God?"* Samuel would pray.

The first son was handsome and strong—he looked like a king! *"No. Do not look at his appearance or physical stature...the Lord does not see as man sees—the Lord looks at the heart,"* answered God. After all the boys had passed before Samuel, he asked if there were any others. Jessie sent for his youngest son, David.

When David was brought to Samuel, God said, *"THIS is the one!"* Samuel anointed David as king. David was a young shepherd boy...and he probably went right back into the fields after being anointed!

Fifteen years passed. During this time period, David fought Goliath. He played the harp for Saul. Saul tried to kill him, and David was on the run. Eventually Saul and his son, Jonathan, died in battle.

David was king of Judah for 7½ years; then he became king of Israel for 33½ years. During his reign, Jerusalem became the capital and Israel became a GREAT NATION. The Tabernacle was brought to Jerusalem, as well as the Ark of the Covenant. During his reign, David realized that he had a grand palace in which to live, but that the Lord only had a tent. He wanted to build a temple to the Lord, but was stopped and told no. David was told by God that his son would build a temple, but David's throne would be established forever.

David's kingdom grew. *"David became greater and greater because the Lord of hosts was with him"* (2 Samuel 5:10). David had *"victory everywhere he went"* (2 Samuel 8:14).

LIFE APPLICATION

■ ■

{Show the candy box of trash.}

The outside of this box looked perfect for its job. It was supposed to hold yummy chocolates. It failed because the outside hid the trash that was on the inside.

{Ask:}

- What type of yucky stuff do people hide inside themselves? [*Sin*]
- What is sin? [*Anything that we think, say, or do that does not please God*]
- What types of sin can go on inside of you that people looking at you would never know about? [*Allow for answers. Lead the children to list sins such as jealousy, envy, hate, selfishness, pride, and other sins that might exist, but never be acted upon.*]
- Does God know your sins that happen inside of you? [*Yes*]

David was known to have a whole heart for God—to be a "man after God's own heart." If you study David's life, you learn that he made a LOT of mistakes. So we know he wasn't perfect.

{Ask:}

- What did God see in David? [*Allow for answers.*]
- What is repentance? [*Knowing you did wrong and choosing to not do that wrong thing again*]

Whenever David sinned against God, in his heart or outwardly, he always accepted the fact that he had wronged God. He agreed with God that he had done wrong and then repented of it.

David truly desired to please God with his whole heart. He was completely committed to God. He was repentant when wrong.

Is the Bible a realistic book? Absolutely. The Bible is honest about the sins of real people. It shows how God uses imperfect people to bring about His perfect plans. David was not perfect. He committed many sins, including murder. But every time God pointed out his sin, David was humble, he repented, and he accepted the punishment and consequences for his actions.

{Show the clear jar.}

God sees straight into your heart. He knows what you think and why you choose to do certain actions. He knows if you want to please Him or if you only want to please yourself.

Therefore, God sent Jesus. He sent Jesus because He knows how yucky our hearts are without Him.

When you desire to please God with your thoughts, words, and actions, then you will produce good fruit. That means you will help God build His Kingdom here on earth. That means you are seeking God's ways and not your own. If you are producing good fruit, then that is proof that Jesus is Master of your heart.

{Show the yucky box.}

We cannot hide our hearts from God. This is what happens when WE are master of our hearts.

{Show the clear jar.}

Every person is transparent to God. He sees what is inside you. When you ask Jesus to clean your heart, He takes all the yuckiness away. He forgives you for your sins and fills you with the Holy Spirit.

- Do we still sin though? [*Yes*]
- You must decide what you want God to see. Do you want new trash in your clear jar? [*Allow for answers.*]
- Or do you want fruit? [*Allow for answers.*]

The Holy Spirit can help you produce fruit if you let Him.

Fruit is sweet. When you produce fruit, not only does it produce a sweet offering to the Lord, but you also show Christ-like behavior towards others.

What can we learn from the anointing of King David? People see the outside, but God sees our hearts. We can either fill our hearts with trash and sin, or we can try to stay clean with the help of the Holy Spirit. Then we please God as we produce fruit.

COMMENT BOX

■ ■

THINK: What went well as you taught this lesson? What can you do better?

_____

_____

_____

_____

_____

_____

_____

_____

_____

TIP: On the Resources Page there is a link to a Fruit of the Spirit lesson.

19 SOLOMON ASKS FOR WISDOM

■ ■

Education is important. But what good is knowing how to do something when you make poor choices? In this object lesson, kids will learn what wisdom is and how to get it. It's not that hard, yet it means going to the Source of wisdom and not doing things OUR way.

Scripture Focus: 1 Kings 3:1-15

Materials:

- A pair of eyeglasses (not sunglasses)
- Graduation cap and/or gown (Dress up so you look "wise.")
- Proverbs 1:7 poster

Geography: Israel, Solomon's kingdom

Knowledge begins with respect for the Lord. But foolish people hate wisdom and discipline.

—Proverbs 1:7 (ICB)

FUTUREFLYINGSAUCERS.COM

Background: King Saul made selfish, disobedient decisions, and Samuel told Saul that God had rejected him as king. Once Saul died, David was king of Judah for 7½ years; then he became king of Israel for 33½ years. During his reign, Jerusalem became the capital and Israel became a GREAT NATION. The Tabernacle was brought to Jerusalem, as well as the Ark of the Covenant. God was with David, who had a whole heart for God. David became great and was given victory after victory. David was a man after God's own heart. Even in the midst of horrible sin, David accepted his shortcomings and the consequences he knew he deserved.

OBJECT LESSON

■ ■

{Ask about the glasses or the outfit you are wearing:}

- Why do people wear robes like this? [*Graduation from high school or college*]
- Graduation is a benchmark event in the lives of people. It means you know something. But do you know everything? [*No*]
- When does a person know everything? [*Allow for answers.*]
- What is the difference between knowledge and wisdom? [*Allow for answers. Knowledge usually indicates knowing facts or how to specifically do something. Wisdom is the ability to make good choices.*]
- Can a person be educated and not be wise? [*Yes*]
- Can a person be uneducated and extremely wise? [*Yes*]

Israel became a GREAT NATION under the kingship of David. However, David was getting old and needed a successor. David chose his son Solomon, the son of Bathsheba, to be his heir to the kingdom. Solomon was a young man, about 20 years old, when David died and Solomon took over the kingdom.

BIBLE LESSON

■ ■

While the Tabernacle was in Jerusalem, the people really did not have a place to worship God. Instead, they would go to the "high places." These were places that were literally higher than the cities, such as mountain tops or hills.

It does not sound bad to us to go to a mountain top and worship the Lord. People today do that all the time. The problem with the Jews going to these high places was that they had been originally used by idol worshipers. The Jews were sacrificing at these high places and not where God wanted them to—the Tabernacle.

Even Solomon, who loved the Lord and walked in His ways had sacrificed at a "high place." One night after Solomon had sacrificed 1,000 burnt offerings, God appeared to Solomon in a dream. God said, *"Ask! What shall I give you?"*

Solomon recognized that he was young and inexperienced and did not know how to be a good king. Solomon asked for an understanding heart, discernment, and wisdom. **The Lord was pleased** and gave Solomon wisdom. He also gave Solomon what he didn't ask for: long life, riches, and success in battle. No one before or after has been as wise as Solomon. The Bible says that Solomon became greater than all the kings of the earth in riches and wisdom. In fact, those who lived across the earth sought out Solomon's wisdom.

{Ask:}

• Why do we need wisdom? [*Allow for answers. Show glasses.*]

Gasses help people to see. Some are nearsighted, which means anything really far away looks fuzzy. Some people are farsighted, which means seeing things up close is difficult. People who have eyes without perfect vision usually wear glasses or contacts.

When I put on my glasses, I can see much more clearly. This is what wisdom does for us. We can be saved, but unless we ask for wisdom, learning from the Bible or dealing with life issues can be fuzzy. The wisdom and discernment of the Holy Spirit allows us to see and learn Scripture and to live a godly life in a crystal-clear way—a way that pleases the Lord and brings Him glory.

{Read Proverbs 1:1-7 aloud.}

These words were written by Solomon, as were the Bible books of Ecclesiastes and Song of Solomon. We have the wisdom of Solomon at our fingertips!

Solomon was wise, but he still made poor decisions out of disobedience. He married MANY women, and those women brought their MANY gods into the nation of Israel. While Solomon always loved the Lord, he did not love Him with his whole heart. Solomon worshiped other idols as well.

Israel truly was a GREAT NATION during the reigns of David and Solomon! God is faithful and His promises are true. In 1 Kings 9:1-7, God appeared to Solomon once more.

{Read Scripture, or have a child read it.}

God gave Solomon an "If...Then" statement. IF you do this, THEN that will happen. Keep in mind, God is ALWAYS faithful and does what He says He is going to do.

{Ask:}

- What actions did God want to see from Solomon? [*Walk before the Lord, have integrity and uprightness, do what God commanded, keep God's laws*]

- If Solomon did those things, what did God promise to do? [*God would establish his throne forever.*]

- What if Solomon and his sons chose NOT to do these actions and chose to follow idols? [*God would cut Israel off from the land and cast them out of His sight.*]

WOW!

IF Solomon walked with God faithfully and was obedient, THEN God would establish his throne forever.

However, IF Solomon and his descendants turned from the Lord and worshiped idols, THEN God would cut off Israel from the land and reject the temple, and Israel would be a name of ridicule.

LIFE APPLICATION

■ ■

Wisdom and obedience work together.

{Ask:}

- Does having wisdom equal being without sin? [*No*]

Even though Solomon was the wisest man in the world, he still sinned and disobeyed God. His reaction to the sin is what mattered to God. David repented and changed his ways. Solomon did not do that.

Putting on the glasses of wisdom will help us to walk in the ways of God. Wisdom is to be valued and sought after. All throughout the Proverbs, wisdom is personified as a woman who desires to give counsel and guidance. I challenge you to read a section of Proverbs each day. Be amazed at the wisdom that God will give you.

What can we learn from Solomon about wisdom? Wisdom is given to us by God. We must ask for it (James 1:5). But we must also obey the One who gives the wisdom to us. If we do not, we can make wise decisions and still destroy ourselves and others with our sin.

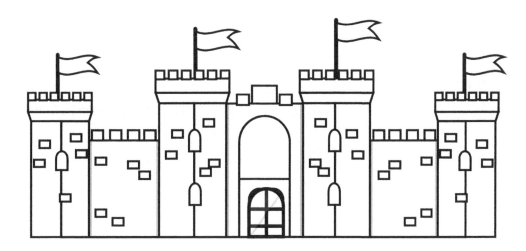

COMMENT BOX

■ ■ ■ ■ ■ ■ ■ ■ ■ ■ ■ ■ ■ ■ ■ ■ ■ ■ ■ ■

THINK: What went well as you taught this lesson? What can you do better?

_____

_____

_____

_____

_____

_____

_____

_____

_____

TIP: There are 31 chapters in the book of Proverbs. Consider reading one chapter per day for the next month.

20 THE DIVIDED KINGDOM OF ISRAEL

■ ■

How important is a nation's leader to the spiritual wellbeing of his nation? In this object lesson, explore that question and the examples of kings, prophets, and the people.

Focus Scripture: 1 Kings 11:28-12:16 (Events toward the end of this lesson come from 1 Kings 14–2 Chronicles. Many interesting things happen during the time of the Divided Kingdom, including adventures of the prophets.)

Materials:

- Dominoes (Try to use the type with straight sides. I used ceramic tiles and they did not work as well.)

- Stable table on which to build a domino pyramid

- 1 Kings 12:15a poster

Geography: Israel, Judah

So the king did not do what the people wanted. The Lord caused this to happen.

—1 Kings 12:15a (ICB)

FUTUREFLYINGSAUCERS.COM

Background: IF Solomon walked with God faithfully and was obedient, THEN God would establish Solomon's throne forever. BUT IF Solomon and his descendants turned from the Lord and worshiped idols, THEN God would cut off Israel from the land and reject the temple, and Israel would be a name of ridicule.

OBJECT LESSON

■ ■

{Stand the dominoes on the longer end to make a pyramid shape. Ask:}

- What happens if I knock over this top domino? [*All the other dominoes will end up falling.*]

{Knock over the domino and have the others fall. As you pick up the dominoes and build the pyramid again, review how God built the nation of Israel. End with Solomon being the king. See the previous lesson for this information. Point to the top domino. Ask:}

- How important is the leader of a nation? [*Allow for answers.*]

- Think about the first kings of Israel: Saul, David, and Solomon. What warning did God continually give them? [*Allow for answers. God continually told them to follow all His commands and to not worship idols.*]

- Why do you think God took these warnings seriously? [*Allow for answers. The leader of a nation will lead by example. If the king worshiped idols, the people would follow.*]

{Tap the first domino again and say, "If the king chose idol worship, then so did most of the people."}

BIBLE LESSON

■ ■

Solomon's heart eventually turned from God. This man whom God gave wisdom, decided to have MANY wives—700 wives, to be exact. AND he had 300 women that he treated as wives, even though they were not. Many of these wives were from other nations with other gods. When they married Solomon, he allowed their gods into Israel and into his heart. He even built altars and temples for these other gods and worshiped them.

Therefore, the Lord became angry with Solomon. God told Solomon that since he had decided to worship other gods, He would tear the kingdom away from him and his sons and give it to a servant. However, because of His love for David, and because of David's heart toward God, He would not do this terrible thing during Solomon's lifetime. God also told Solomon that He would not take away the entire kingdom from Solomon's family. Solomon's sons would get to keep a kingdom of one tribe instead of all twelve tribes.

Sometime after this, God spoke through the prophet Ahijah to Solomon's servant named Jeroboam. The prophet had on a new cloak. He took it off and tore it into 12 pieces. Ahijah told Jeroboam to pick up 10 pieces of the cloak. God told Jeroboam he would receive 10 tribes of the kingdom and that if he obeyed God's commands, God would be with him. Solomon somehow found out about the prophecy and wanted to put Jeroboam to death. Jeroboam fled to Egypt.

{Build the domino pyramid again.}

Solomon died and his son, Rehoboam, became king. The people of Israel, including Jeroboam (who had returned from Egypt), came to the new king and asked if he would lighten the yoke that was on them. Rehoboam called all of his father's advisers and elders to ask them how he should run the kingdom. Solomon had taxed the people quite a bit, and the elders advised Rehoboam to lighten up on the people. Rehoboam then went to his younger advisers and asked them what to do. They told him to tax the people even more. Rehoboam rejected the advice of the elders and told the people, *"My little finger will be thicker than my father's waist!"* He also told them he would punish with whips and scourges.

Therefore, Jeroboam replied, *"To your tents, oh Israel!"*

Rehoboam prepared for civil war. He wanted to fight, but God stopped him and said, *"This thing is from Me!"* Rehoboam obeyed and did not fight, which allowed 10 of the tribes to side with Jeroboam to form the nation of Israel. Rehoboam was left with the lands of Judah, forming the nation of Judah. (Levi does not really count because the Levites had cities all over the nation.) The GREAT NATION was divided.

Jeroboam did not want people traveling to Jerusalem to offer sacrifices to God because then they might not return. So he built altars and temples to God and other gods in his nation. Jeroboam was not obedient to the Lord, and this began years of turmoil and consequences for these tribes.

{Tap the top domino again.}

LIFE APPLICATION

■ ■

{Ask:}

• Do the personal beliefs of a nation's leader matter? [*Allow for answers.*]

Yes, a leader's personal beliefs matter. Over and over God tells the leaders, "*If you will obey Me... then I will be with you!*" We see in this tragic and sad bit of history what happens when a nation's leader does not obey the Lord.

Throughout the books of Chronicles and the prophets, we see civil war and unrest. We see offerings made to other gods. We see people involved in horrible sin.

The heart of a leader leads him, and he leads those under him. Eventually, the leader changes the people of a nation—not all the people, though. Many of the kings during the time of the Divided Kingdom were evil, but we learn about people like Elijah, Elisha, and Isaiah. Those prophets chose to obey God rather than the kings. Those whose hearts totally belong to God can withstand any leader.

Let us be sure to participate any time we might be able to help select our leaders.

What can we learn from the Divided Kingdom? The leader of a nation influences the spiritual growth of the people under him. The leader can be for God or against Him. We need to pray for our leaders.

COMMENT BOX

■ ■

THINK: What went well as you taught this lesson? What can you do better?

_____

_____

_____

_____

_____

_____

_____

_____

_____

TIP: The nation of Israel had zero kings who loved God. The nation of Judah had eight. If you have older children, have them read about Josiah or Hezekiah to see what happens when a king reflects God.

21 ZERUBBABEL REBUILDS THE TEMPLE

■ ■

Sometimes being a Christ-follower is difficult because we can be mocked and discouraged by other people. Use this Bible lesson about Zerubbabel to teach children that when God gives them a task to do, it is much better to obey Him than to listen to discouraging people.

Focus Scripture: Ezra 4

Materials:

- Blocks of numerous sizes and shapes
- Small table
- Zechariah 4:6 poster

Geography: Persia, Jerusalem

Then he told me, "This is the message from the Lord to Zerubbabel: 'You will not succeed by your own strength or by your own power. The power will come from my Spirit,' says the Lord of heaven's armies."

—Zechariah 4:6 (ICB)

Background: The people of Israel split into two kingdoms. The Northern Kingdom of Israel had no kings that feared the Lord. In time, Israel's enemies conquered them and scattered those tribes throughout the known world. The Southern Kingdom of Judah had eight kings who followed the ways of the Lord. Because of this, God's mercy was extended for a time.

However, eventually all of the people and the leaders went after other gods, and the One True God allowed the people of Judah to be exiled to Babylon. The Israelites, or Hebrews, were now called *Jews* because they had come from the kingdom of Judah.

OBJECT LESSON

■ ■

{Have the blocks on the table. Allow a child to build a tower. When the tower is partially built, shake the table so that the tower falls down. Tell the child to build the tower again. Again, when the tower is partially built, shake the tower so that it falls down. At this point the child might be irritated with you. Allow him to choose a partner to see if they can get the tower built. Again, shake the table so that it falls down.}

{Ask:}

- What job did I give you to do? [*Build a tower*]

- Were you able to build it? [*No*]

- Why? [*Allow for answers.*]

- How did you feel when I stopped you from building? [*Allow for answers.*]

BIBLE LESSON

■ ■

Do you remember Daniel and the lion's den (Daniel 6)? Daniel was a young man when King Nebuchadnezzar destroyed Jerusalem, took all the riches from the Temple, and then destroyed it. For 70 years the Jews were in captivity throughout the kingdom of Babylon. When Daniel was an old man, Babylon was attacked and defeated by the Persian Empire.

A new king, King Cyrus, was on the throne. King Cyrus made a proclamation allowing the Jews to go back to Jerusalem and rebuild the Temple. The king also gave the people all of the gold and riches that King Nebuchadnezzar had taken from the Temple.

Zerubbabel helped to lead those Jews who wanted to return to Jerusalem. After 70 years, many of the Jews who had been born in captivity enjoyed their Babylonian lives. A large number did not want to return to Jerusalem. About 42,000 Jews returned to rebuild the temple. Jerusalem was still under the rule of Persia, but the king was allowing them to go home!

However, there were people already living in the land of Israel. Some of the people were poor Jews who had been left behind, and they had intermarried with Gentiles. These people were called Samaritans. Others were Canaanites. When the Jews returned, they were not welcome.

The Jews were determined to do what God wanted them to do: rebuild the Temple. When they arrived, some older people wept because they remembered the splendor of Solomon's Temple before it was destroyed.

The foundations of the Temple were there, so the people began to rebuild it.

The Canaanites and Samaritans did not approve. They tried to discourage, frustrate, and threaten the people as they began to build.

{Ask:}

- Remember how you felt when the blocks kept falling? [*Yes*]
- How do you think the Jews felt? [*Allow for answers.*]

The enemies of the Jews eventually wrote a letter to a new Persian king, Artaxerxes. They could get the king to stop the building of the temple.

About 15 years went by. No one worked on the temple. The Jews were too afraid.

Two prophets began to encourage the people. One was Haggai, who represented the older generation; the other was Zechariah, who represented the younger Jews. Both encouraged the people to do what the Lord had originally told them to do: rebuild the temple.

And the Jews did. They started the building project again, and once again those in the land didn't like it. However, "the eye of God" was upon the Jews. Even though the people of the land sent a letter to another new king, Darius, the Jews did not stop building.

Eventually a letter arrived from King Darius, and he proclaimed that the Jews had permission to continue and finish building the Temple.

The Temple was completed!

{Allow the child to return to the blocks and rebuild the structure. Celebrate when it is completed, just as the Jews celebrated when their temple was completed.}

LIFE APPLICATION

■ ■

God has a plan for your life. He has given you gifts and abilities.

{Ask:}

- What do you want to be when you grow up? [*Allow for answers.*]

Those are great goals. However, if God hasn't told you to do those things, you will be wasting your time. The Jews were given a specific task. God will give you a task as well. Through prayer and learning, God will reveal to you what He wants you to do when you grow up. It will be an adventure!

There will be times when other people are not going to agree with the task God gives you. Like the people of the land discouraged the Jews, you might have people in your life who discourage you from doing what God wants you to do.

{Ask:}

- Which is more important, to do what God tells you to do or to do what people tell you? [*What God tells you*]
- Are there wise people you can listen to who can help you know what God wants you to do? [*Yes*]
- How can you respond to those who might not agree with what you are doing for God? [*Allow for answers. Guide them to realize that they can be polite, and still do what God tells them to do. Also help them to see that sometimes following God means being treated poorly by others, like the Jews were.*]
- How do you know what God wants you to do? [*Read the Bible; pray and listen to His voice.*]

While Jesus was on earth, He was mocked for things that He did. He healed on the Sabbath. He said things against the religious leaders. He was silent when accused of blasphemy. He was mocked while dying on the cross. If we choose to be Jesus followers, then we must expect that we will be made fun of at some point in time.

What can we learn from Zerubbabel rebuilding the temple? The Bible is filled with commands and actions that we should be doing. Sometimes other people won't like it when we do what God wants us to do. We can be strong and courageous and do what God wants anyway. We answer to Him, not to people.

COMMENT BOX

THINK: What went well as you taught this lesson? What can you do better?

_____

_____

_____

_____

_____

_____

_____

_____

_____

TIP: See the Resources Page for a link to learn interesting facts about Zerubbabel's Temple.

22 ESTHER'S COURAGE

■ ■

Being a Christ-follower can be difficult because sometimes we might be persecuted for what we believe. Use this Bible lesson about Esther to teach children that God gives us faith and courage to handle any situation when we trust entirely in Him.

Focus Scripture: Esther 4

Materials:

- Ceiling fan or ceiling tiles
- String or yarn
- Tennis ball, or other soft ball (Tie the string around the tennis ball. Hang the ball from the ceiling using the string. The ball should hang two to three feet from the floor. Be sure to have room for the ball to swing in the room.)
- Esther 4:14 poster

Geography: Persia, Susa

Background: The people of the Northern Kingdom had been scattered by the Assyrians. Those of the Southern Kingdom were taken into

"You might keep quiet at this time. Then someone else will help and save the Jews. But you and your father's family will all die. And who knows, you may have been chosen queen for just such a time as this."

—Esther 4:14 (ICB)

FUTUREFLYINGSAUCERS.COM

captivity by the Babylonians. After 70 years, Zerubbabel took the first group of Jews back to Israel from Babylon and rebuilt the temple because of a decree made by the new Persian king. Thirty-eight years after the temple was completed, a young Jewess named Esther found favor with the next Persian king and was crowned queen of all Babylon.

OBJECT LESSON

■ ■

{Choose a volunteer. Have the person stand about two feet away from the hanging tennis ball so that when the ball is pulled toward them it will reach their chin. The string should stay straight.}

{Ask:}

- Do you trust me? [*Allow answers. The child will probably say yes, and then not be so sure once you say what you are going to do.*]

{As you hold the tennis ball to the volunteer's chin, explain that you want the volunteer to stand still while you drop the ball. Ask:}

- When I drop this ball, what will happen? [*Allow answers. The children should think that the ball will swing away and then come back to hit the face of the volunteer.*]

{Proceed to drop the ball. It should swing away and then come back to the face of the volunteer, but not as near as where you dropped it. This is an example of periodic motion with a pendulum. The volunteer might squint his or her eyes as the ball comes close again before realizing that there was never any danger. Warning: All the kids will want to try this when you are finished! Ask:}

- Even though you trusted me, were you a little scared the ball might hit you in the face? [*Yes*]

- Did it take courage for you to stand here even if you were a little scared? [*Yes*]

Trust, faith, and courage all work together to help us glorify the Lord. A little bit of fear and adrenaline is a part of the Christian life. This is what makes being a Christian so exciting!

BIBLE LESSON

■ ■

{Introduce the main characters of this historical event. When you introduce Haman, tell the kids to boo and hiss one time whenever they hear his name. Make sure to tell them it should be a short boo and hiss, or else your story-telling will take quite a while! You might want to practice once or twice so the kids know your expectations.}

The people of this historical event include Mordecai the Jew; his niece Hadassah (Hebrew name) or Esther (Persian name); the king; and Haman. (Boo! Hiss!)

The Persian king decided to look for a new queen after his first one disobeyed his commands. He held a beauty pageant, and all of the eligible girls of the kingdom were to be in it. The king chose a young girl named Esther. Her cousin Mordecai had told her to hide the fact that she was a Jew and to be called by her Persian name instead of her Hebrew name.

The King's right-hand man was Haman. (Boo! Hiss!) He enjoyed his high position quite a bit. Haman (Boo! Hiss!) even expected the people of Susa to bow down to him when he walked by.

One man would not though...Mordecai. He never would bow down when Haman (Boo! Hiss!) went by. Mordecai the Jew believed in the One True God and thought that only He should be bowed down to.

This made Haman (Boo! Hiss!) extremely mad. It made him so mad that he wanted to kill Mordecai—and not just Mordecai, but all the Jews.

Haman (Boo! Hiss!) explained to the king that the Jews did not follow the king's laws, but instead followed their own laws. He convinced the king that these people should be destroyed. The king allowed Haman (Boo! Hiss!) to write the edict which proclaimed that on a certain day, all people in the kingdom could attack the Jews—men, women, and children—and annihilate them and take all of their possessions.

When Mordecai heard about the edict, he tore his clothes in grief and cried bitter cries. Esther heard about Mordecai and sent a servant to find out what was wrong. Mordecai told him about Haman's (Boo! Hiss!) edict. After the servant told Esther, she sent a message to Mordecai that said, *"Anyone knows that if a person chooses to go into the king's presence without being summoned, that person will be put to death unless the king is pleased and holds out his scepter. The king has not asked to see me in thirty days."*

Mordecai sent a message back saying: *"Do you really think you will escape death anyway? You are Jewish! If you stay silent, you will be killed and another person will be used to save the Jews. Who knows? Maybe you were placed where you are for such a time as this!"*

Esther told Mordecai to have the people fast for three days.

On the third day, Esther dressed in her royal robes and went to see the king. She found favor in his eyes. The king held out his scepter and asked her what she wanted.

Esther invited the king and Haman (Boo! Hiss!) to a dinner party.

At the dinner party, the king asked Esther what she wanted...and she asked for them to come to dinner again the next night.

The next night the king asked Esther what she would like. Esther answered, *"If it pleases the King, please give me my life and the lives of my people, for we are going to be destroyed."*

The king was angered and wanted to know who would do such a thing. Esther told him: Haman! (Boo! Hiss!)

The king's first edict could not be stopped. Instead, the king issued another decree stating that the Jewish people could arm themselves against their enemies and fight those who attacked them.

So they did.

LIFE APPLICATION

■ ■

{Ask:}

- What feelings do you think Esther felt when Mordecai told her about the king's first decree? [*Allow for answers.*]

- How do you think she felt when she realized she would have to go see the king? [*Allow for answers.*]

- Have you ever watched a friend or a stranger be treated unfairly or in a mean way? [*Allow for answers.*]

- What did you do? [*Allow for answers.*]

- What could you have done? [*Allow for answers. Lead the children to see that standing up for those who are being bullied is good. They could have told an adult, or even stepped in to help the person who was being treated wrongly. Discuss that choosing to do the right thing can be scary.*]

- The name of God is never mentioned in the book of Esther. But what did she ask Mordecai to do? [*Fast*]

- What is fasting? [*Fasting, in this case, was choosing to go without food or drink to show grief and to pray.*]

- Do you think Esther trusted God to help her? [*Yes*]

Because Esther had faith in God, she chose to trust Him with her life. She went before the king to stand up for her people who were going to be killed. Because of her trust, God blessed her with courage. And because of her courage, she saved the lives of her people.

Jesus asks us to do some pretty crazy things such as forgiving people (Matthew 18:21-22) or treating people the same way we would want to be treated (Matthew 7:12). He wants us to be kind and merciful to people. He wants us to love others who are different than us (John 13:34). He wants us to help those who are poor or who are being treated badly (John 14:12).

{Ask:}

- Do you think it might take courage to do some of the things Jesus asks us to do? [*Yes*]

- How can you get courage to do the right thing? [*Lead the children to understand that we must believe in Jesus first, then we can trust Him and ask Him for courage when we need it.*]

What can we learn from Esther? When we believe God is who He says He is, then we can trust Him fully. When we trust in a powerful God who loves us and cares for us, then we can ask for the courage we need to do the hard things Jesus asks us to do that might cause us to be frightened.

COMMENT BOX

■ ■

THINK: What went well as you taught this lesson? What can you do better?

_____

_____

_____

_____

_____

_____

_____

_____

_____

_____

TIP: Throughout the ages, enemies have tried to destroy the Jewish nation. However, Jesus still needed to come. Even after Jesus rose from the dead, the Jews were hated. The Bible tells us that those who do not harm the Jews will be blessed by the Lord (Genesis 12:3). The Jews are God's chosen people. Christians are adopted into that family. Be sure to teach that we should support those of the Jewish faith through prayer (Psalm 122:6) and the giving of material needs (Romans 15:27).

23 SKITTLES, WATER, AND EZRA

■ ■

When a person is in the middle of a sinful situation, it is hard to make correct choices. Use Skittles and warm water for this object lesson to teach children that God's commands are for our protection.

**NOTE: This section of Scripture can be hard for kids to hear, especially for those who are in divorced families. Sometimes Scripture does not make sense to us humans. We know that God is good and loves families. It is important to remember that God has a HUGE plan we know little of... AND that His objective is to get rid of sin so He can be glorified. Be sensitive to those kids who might have questions about their own families after this lesson. Be sure to reassure them that all people and families can be redeemed through Jesus Christ.

"But now, our God, what can we say after you have done all this? We have disobeyed your commands."
—Ezra 9:10 (ICB)

FUTUREFLYINGSAUCERS.COM

Focus Scripture: Ezra 9-10

Materials:

- White dinner plate
- 20-25 Skittles
- Warm water (I used hot tap water.)
- Ezra 9:10 poster

Geography: Persia, Jerusalem

Background: Zerubbabel returned to Jerusalem with many of the exiled Jews and rebuilt the temple. Afterwards, Esther, a Jewess who was a Persian queen, saved her people from annihilation. Twenty years later, Ezra brought another large group of Jews back to Jerusalem.

OBJECT LESSON

■ ■

{In advance, place the Skittles around the plate, creating a large circle. Put on a flat surface for best results. With the kids, pour the warm water in the middle of the Skittles, enough so that the liquid just about covers the candy. Watch what happens!}

These Skittles were untouched and perfect candies when first put on the plate.

{After about 2-3 minutes, ask:}

• What happened when the water touched the candy? [*The colors of the candy bled.*]

{Take your finger and mix the colors. A brown-red color should appear. Ask:}

• What happened when I mixed the pretty colors? [*A dark, yucky color appeared.*]

The colors stayed pretty for a time, and then they turned yucky. That's what happens with sin. It looks good to us at the beginning, but once we do the sin, and then do it again and again....then our lives get yucky.

BIBLE LESSON

■■■■■■■■■■■■■■■■■■■■■■■■■

That's what happened with the Jews. Zerubbabel took back a group of people to Jerusalem to rebuild the temple. Once the temple was built, the people came and worshiped God. They began to celebrate the feasts and offer sacrifices once more.

The Samaritans in the land had given Zerubbabel a tough time about building the temple, mainly because they worshiped idols. The Samaritans were a people group who were part Jew and part Canaanite. They had turned from God's law to not marry into other people groups.

{Ask:}

- Why would God not want His chosen people to marry those who were not Jews? [*Allow for answers. God had given strict rules to the Jews to only marry Jews because He knew that other people groups worshiped idols. He also knew that if the Jews began to intermarry, then those who were not Jews would bring their idol worship into Jewish families. Then children would not be taught about the One True God, but about idols.*]

As the years passed, the Jews began to marry women and men who were not Jews. God sent Ezra, a priest and scribe who sought God, to Jerusalem. He took another large group of Jews with him. The Persian king also gave Ezra treasures for the temple treasury—an offering of sorts. Ezra also made sure many Levites and priests returned as well. Ezra wanted to be sure that the temple had plenty of people to run it.

Ezra was a man who sought the Law of the Lord and was determined to follow it. He was also prepared to teach the people God's Law.

After Ezra arrived in Jerusalem and put the treasures in the temple, the leaders of the people told Ezra that some of the Jews—even some of the priests and Levites—had intermarried with Canaanites.

Ezra was distraught! He ripped his clothes, pulled his beard, and sat down totally stunned by this news. Before the evening sacrifice, Ezra fell face down before the Lord.

Ezra prayed, *"Oh, God! I am ashamed to lift my face to you! I am humiliated because of the sins that are higher than my head! We are guilty! For a little while you have given grace. For you have told us to not give our sons and daughters in marriage to those who are unclean. Lord, only You are righteous!"*

While Ezra prayed, a large gathering of people showed up in the temple, and they were weeping because of their sin. A leader stood up and cried loudly for all to hear, *"We have sinned against God and taken pagan wives. Let us make a covenant with God to put away these wives and their children."*

Ezra stood up, and the people decided that those men who had married pagan women would confess to Ezra and a few other leaders who had NOT taken pagan wives. Then those pagan wives and their children would have to leave and go back to the towns from which they came.

The people obeyed.

LIFE APPLICATION

■ ■ ■ ■ ■ ■ ■ ■ ■ ■ ■ ■ ■ ■ ■ ■ ■ ■ ■ ■

It is hard for us to believe that God would be pleased by the breaking up of all these families. Yet, God is not pleased with sin. Sin spreads and affects everyone. Those marriages were started in disobedience, and idols became the norm. Therefore, in THIS particular situation, it was in the best interest for the Jews that these women and children return to the Canaanite villages.

Can families that are soaked in sin be redeemed? YES! But it means getting rid of the sin. In this case with the Jews, the only way to get rid of the idol worship was to get rid of those who were worshiping the idols.

{Ask:}

- What should have happened so families would not have been broken apart? [*Allow for answers. Lead children to see that if the men had married Jewish women as God had commanded, then the intermarriage issue never would have happened.*]

God chose the Jews to be His holy people, a nation set apart from the rest of the world. If the Jews intermarried, then everyone in the household had to follow the Jewish faith (such as Ruth and Rahab). Many times, the wives or husbands of other races brought their own gods into the house. This caused those families to no longer be set apart. They were mixed, like the Skittles. The mixing of Jewish life and idol worship led to even more sin. (Remember Solomon?)

The same thing can happen to us. If you choose to be a Jesus-follower, a Christian, then you are to be set apart. Christians live life by God's rules, not the world's rules. That means we make different choices.

{Ask:}

- What choices should a Christian make that are different than what an unbeliever might do? [*Allow for answers. Possible answers could include: telling the truth all the time, no matter what; staying away from drinking and drugs; choosing to hang out with friends who also love Jesus; choosing to walk out of a movie if it includes nudity or foul language or glorifies evil; choosing to not marry an unbeliever.*]

It is important for you to go ahead and think about what you would do if you were in these diverse types of scenarios. When you are in the middle of a tempting situation and have no plan, then you will almost certainly choose to sin.

However, if you decide now to hang out with people who love Jesus, then that will save you a lot of trouble in the future.

{Ask:}

- Does this mean we never speak to, or do anything with, people who are not saved? [*No*]

We absolutely should have friends who do not know Jesus, and we should spend time with those who do not go to church. However, we should not spend most of our time with them. Most of your time should be with those who love Jesus.

There is one command, though, that we need to follow. 2 Corinthians 6:14 tells us to not join with those who do not believe. This command is talking about making commitments.

If you are a Christian, then go ahead and decide now not to marry anyone who is not a Christian. In fact, do not even date someone who is not a practicing Christian. Pray for your future spouse.

Do not go into business with someone who is not a believer because a business contract is like a marriage. You want to be able to trust a business partner. Your reputations are united.

God does not give us commands like this to make us miserable. He gives us commands so we will not have to deal with the trouble these particular sins can cause. God loves you. He always wants what is best for you. He wants you to stay away from situations that can hurt you. He is jealous for you.

What can we learn from Ezra? God takes sin seriously and gives us loving commands that protect us if we choose to obey them.

COMMENT BOX

■ ■

THINK: What went well as you taught this lesson? What can you do better?

_____

_____

_____

_____

_____

_____

_____

_____

_____

TIP: This is a good opportunity to talk about praying for family members. Many families have one parent who may not have a relationship with Jesus. 1 Corinthians 7:12-16 gives some guidance for these types of marriages.

24 NEHEMIAH BUILDS THE WALL

■■■■■■■■■■■■■■■■■■■■■■■■

What does it mean to be successful? This lesson about Nehemiah building the wall discusses this question and how obedience to God brings success.

Focus Scripture: Nehemiah 6

Materials:

- Small drinking cups or larger plastic party cups (You will need 15-20 cups per child.)
- Nehemiah 6:16 poster

Geography: Jerusalem

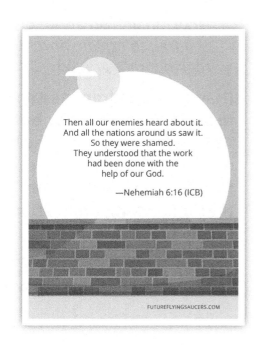

Then all our enemies heard about it. And all the nations around us saw it. So they were shamed. They understood that the work had been done with the help of our God.

—Nehemiah 6:16 (ICB)

FUTUREFLYINGSAUCERS.COM

Background: Zerubbabel returned with many of the exiled Jews to Jerusalem and rebuilt the temple. Afterwards, Esther, a Jewess who was a Persian queen, saved her people from annihilation. Twenty years later, Ezra brought another large group of Jews back to Jerusalem.

OBJECT LESSON

■ ■

{Give each child a stack of 15-20 cups, depending upon how many kids you have. Have the children get into groups of 5 or 6. Tell them to sit in a circle, knee to knee, and then turn around with their backs toward each other. Have them scoot back until their knees are close together again. Everyone should be facing outside the circle.

Tell them to use their cups to build a wall around themselves. They must work with the person on either side of them to make sure that the sections of cups are connected. They will need to realize that they must communicate with each other to make sure the height is the same all the way around. When the wall is built, celebrate!}

{Ask:}

- How did you go about building your cup wall? [*Allow for answers. Lead the children to explain how they worked with those next to them and how they worked together as a group.*]

{Have the children take down their wall sections. Explain that they are going to build the wall again, but that this time, you might do something different. Tell them to begin. As the kids are building, choose one and ask him to stand up, turn around one time, and sit down. Then choose another child. Have her stand up, clap five times, and sit down. Do this continuously. Act shocked that it is taking them SO much longer to build the wall this time. When they finally finish, ask:}

- Why did it take you longer to build the wall this time? [*Allow for answers, but they might be frustrated with you and blame you!*]

BIBLE LESSON

■ ■

Zerubbabel built the temple, and many Jews moved back to Jerusalem. However, there was still no wall that protected the people.

Ezra was a scribe who returned to Jerusalem to help reestablish God's Law in the city. About 10 years later, Nehemiah returned to Jerusalem. He had permission from the king of Persia to rebuild the walls around Jerusalem.

Nehemiah was the cupbearer for the king of Persia. A cupbearer had an important job. He tasted all of the food and drink before the king ate any of it. This was a poison check! Being the cupbearer might have meant that Nehemiah was a security force in the kitchens and around the palace. He was a slave, but he was an important slave. Safety was a real concern for him, and he was totally trusted by the king.

When he arrived, Nehemiah was concerned about the safety of the people of Jerusalem. He wanted to build a wall as quickly as possible. Each family, or clan, of Jews built a certain section of the wall. Therefore, the wall was being built around Jerusalem all at the same time.

Many people were against the Jews rebuilding the walls—especially the Samaritans and the Canaanites. Just like they had fought Zerubbabel, they fought against Nehemiah as well. The threats from these enemies caused the people who were building the wall to wear swords and other weapons while they rebuilt.

Nehemiah continued to encourage the people. The walls continued to grow taller. The Canaanite leaders tried various kinds of tricks to get the Jews to stop building.

When the wall was almost completed, a messenger from the Canaanite leaders went to Nehemiah. The message said, *"Come meet with us!"* but Nehemiah told them no.

The Canaanite leaders sent another message: *"Come meet with us!"*

Nehemiah responded, *"No, I am doing a great work. I will not come down to you."*

This made the Canaanite leaders upset. After two or three more messages like those, they sent another message saying, *"There is a rumor that you are building a wall so that YOU can be the king. We hear prophets saying that you are going to be king. Therefore, we are going to go tell the king of Persia this report."*

Nehemiah responded saying, *"There is no such thing going on."*

Nehemiah ignored the threats from these men. So they tried something else.

There was a man in town named Shemaiah. He was an informant for the Canaanite leaders. He went to Nehemiah and said, *"Go to the Temple. Someone is going to try to take your life!"*

There was a rule that if a person's life was threatened, then he could enter the Temple and hold on to the horns of the altar of sacrifice. If he did this, then his life would be spared.

Nehemiah thought about this. It does not sound bad to go to the Temple. However, there were only certain parts of the Temple that regular men could go to. Nehemiah was not a priest or a Levite. It was possible Shemaiah was trying to get Nehemiah to go to a part of the Temple that was off limits to Nehemiah.

Nehemiah responded to Shemaiah and said that God would protect him. God allowed Nehemiah to know that this man had claimed a false prophecy and that there had been other prophets saying false prophecies as well.

The wall was finished being built after 52 days. When all the Canaanite leaders heard this, they were disheartened. They knew that all the work had been done by God. It was unheard of that walls would be built in such a short amount of time.

LIFE APPLICATION

■ ■

{Ask:}

- Remember the cup wall that you built. How did Nehemiah handle being distracted? [*He had the people protect themselves against the threats and he ignored the other leaders. He was focused on the task God had given to him.*]

- What types of things might distract you from coming to church? [*Allow for answers.*]

- What types of things might distract you from reading your Bible? [*Allow for answers.*]

- What types of things might distract you from praying? [*Allow for answers.*]

- What might distract you from making righteous decisions? [*Allow for answers.*]

- How can you be like Nehemiah in those situations? [*Make God a priority, focus on reading or praying, know which choices are righteous and do them, etc.*]

Our enemy, Satan, would LOVE for you to be distracted instead of spending time with God. He does not want you to have protection. He does not want you to grow spiritually.

Satan knows that the more you read your Bible, the more you pray, and the more you listen to God, the higher your wall of protection against sin will be. You will make much better decisions when you are focused on God.

Jesus was a busy person, yet He chose to take out sections of time to focus on God. He would get away from His disciples and those who followed Him around, and He would pray. So if Jesus needed to communicate with God the Father, how much more should we.

Jesus knew He had a specific purpose given to Him by God. Nehemiah knew he had a specific purpose given to him by God. Nehemiah was successful. Jesus was successful.

YOU have a specific purpose given to YOU by God. Stay focused on the One Who can help you do the great work! And YOU will be successful!

What can we learn from Nehemiah? Distractions will always be around us, so we need to figure out how to stay focused on God. When we stay focused on God and His plan, we will be successful no matter what!

COMMENT BOX

THINK: What went well as you taught this lesson? What can you do better?

_____

_____

_____

_____

_____

_____

_____

_____

TIP: What distracts you from your quiet time and study with God? Be intentional to stick with a flexible Bible reading and prayer schedule.

25 THE TIME BETWEEN THE TESTAMENTS

◼◼◼◼◼◼◼◼◼◼◼◼◼◼◼◼◼◼◼

Waiting...it can be hard to do. Why is it important to know what happened in history between the Old and New Testaments? Use a fun science experiment to discuss waiting and what God was doing between the Old and New Testaments.

Scripture Focus: Galatians 4:4

Materials:

- Balloon
- Water bottle
- Water
- Baking soda
- Citric acid (found in the canning section of the grocery store)
- Galatians 4:4 poster

Geography: Greece, Rome, Israel

Background: The Old Testament was over. This was the time between the books of Malachi and Matthew. God became silent.

But when the right time came, God sent his Son. His Son was born of a woman and lived under the law.

—Galatians 4:4 (ICB)

FUTUREFLYINGSAUCERS.COM

OBJECT LESSON

■ ■

{Prepare before the lesson: Use a half-filled water bottle. Add one tsp. (5.69 g) of citric acid to the bottle. Carefully add one tsp. (5.69 g) of baking soda to the inside of the balloon. I used a funnel made from an index card.}

{Ask:}

- Tell me about a time when you have been SO excited for something to happen that it was hard to wait. [*Allow for answers.*]

- Can you think of people in the Bible who may have had a hard time waiting for God to do something? [*Allow for answers. Examples: Noah, Abraham, Sarah, Moses, Hannah, Elizabeth, Zachariah*]

Waiting can be hard, especially if you are waiting for something that you know will be good!

We are going to do an experiment. We need to fill up this balloon, but we are not going to blow it up ourselves. We could do that very fast. Instead we are going to have the bottle fill up the balloon and we will not even need to touch it. BUT! We will have to wait for the balloon to fill. If it fills up, what a NEAT and FUN experiment we did!

{Take the balloon and carefully wrap the opening over the bottle opening. Quickly lift up the balloon, dump in the baking soda, and drop the balloon down again so you aren't touching the experiment. WAIT! The balloon should fill up with carbon dioxide gas.}

After waiting, the balloon filled up! We did not have to wait TOO long though—at least not like the Israelites did. They knew their Messiah was supposed to come. They waited...and they waited...

In fact, the Old Testament ended. The exile had ended. Those Jews who wanted to return to Israel had returned. And so they waited.

BIBLE LESSON

■ ■

Four hundred years take place between the end of the Old Testament and the beginning of the New Testament. In the Old Testament, God did many things to prepare the world for His salvation process. Throughout the Old Testament, God spoke to people. He did amazing wonders. He built a nation.

After the book of Malachi, God became silent. As far as we know, God did not speak to anyone during those years, or at least no one wrote it down.

God was still at work. He was working...and doing a lot. Let's have a brief history lesson and learn some vocabulary!

Many Powers: Countries seem to enjoy fighting over land. People today are STILL fighting over the land of Israel. During the time between the Old and New Testaments, at least three powerful countries rose to power. The first was Persia. Persia allowed the Jews to keep their religion. Remember, the king of Persia allowed Nehemiah to rebuild the walls of Jerusalem, and the people rebuilt the temple. Ezra brought back the Word of God. During the first 100 years of the 400 years of silence, Israel was at peace with the surrounding nations with Persia in control. The Jews did their own thing.

Greece Brings One Language: Then Alexander the Great came along and conquered lands for Greece, including Israel. They forced people to speak Greek, which allowed for people in different countries to communicate with each other. Greece also wanted to spread their polytheistic culture (worshiping many gods), and the Jews did not like that. One thing they learned from exile was that they were a nation with ONE God and one God ONLY. They were not going to make that mistake again.

Israel has Hopes: The culture of that day, in the eyes of the Jews, was worldly and sinful. The Jews knew that they were a nation specifically created by God for a specific reason. They considered those who surrounded them as evil unclean people. There were Jews and there were Gentiles. People were clean or unclean. All the Jews could do was hope their Messiah would come soon and get them away from the unrighteous nations.

Rome Builds Roads: Greece weakened and Rome conquered them. This was the time of Pax Romana, Romans Peace. There was peace because if the conquered peoples did not cooperate, then they would be executed. (Ever heard of crucifixion?) So this was a time of relative peace and building. The Romans built buildings and bath houses, aqueducts and roads. Once roads were built, transportation was much easier.

Politics: Though Israel was governed by Caesar, it had its own leadership issues.

Sanhedrin: This was the governing religious body that was a mix of Sadducees and Pharisees. This was the group that made "laws" and judged the Jewish people for religious matters.

Scribes: These were men who, by hand, made copies of the Holy Scriptures.

Sadducees: This was a religious political group that accepted only the five books of Moses as the Law. They did not believe in resurrection. They held a lot of power in the Sanhedrin.

Pharisees: This was the opposing political group of the Sadducees. This group accepted the Law of Moses and added additional oral laws to their teachings. This meant they followed a bunch of rules that were not a part of Scripture.

Publicans: These men were also known as tax collectors. They were usually Jews who collected money for Rome, while stealing the riches of their own people. These men were greatly despised and seen as traitors by the people of Israel.

Zealots: These people were ready to attack the Romans, but they were waiting for the Messiah to come and join them. In the meantime, they would attack Roman soldiers and attempt to overthrow local leadership.

LIFE APPLICATION

■ ■

Why is all this important? God never spoke. What was going on?

He didn't speak...but He was DOING.

Just like we had to wait for the balloon to fill, God was working and waiting to begin His salvation process. The world wasn't ready until all of these things happened in history.

Just because God did not speak and have someone write down His words does not mean He was not actively present and at work. The world was going through the motions of life, but God was preparing it for a Messiah. The fact that there was a common language would help people understand the Word of God. Safe, good roads meant that the Word of God would be able to easily travel. God was setting the stage for salvation!

When the time was right, a certain angel appeared to a certain woman in the specific town of Bethlehem.

Let the New Testament begin!

What can we learn from the time between the Old and New Testaments? God is always at work around us even if we don't see or hear Him. He cares about the details of your life and has a specific plan for you.

COMMENT BOX

■ ■

THINK: What went well as you taught this lesson? What can you do better?

_____

_____

_____

_____

_____

_____

_____

_____

_____

TIP: When this experiment starts to bubble, some of the liquid comes up into the balloon. Don't pour the baking soda in too fast, but if the bubbles do get into the balloon, dump the water back into the bottle and the carbon dioxide should fill the balloon.

BONUS
BONUS

BONUS

THE BIRTH OF JESUS

■■■■■■■■■■■■■■■■■■■■■■■■■■■

Christmas is about Jesus. He's the main character. But sometimes focusing on the lesser known people can teach us a lot. This object lesson focuses on Joseph and his role in an event that brought salvation to the world.

Scripture Focus: Matthew 1:18-25

Materials:

- Gold, black, red, white, and green poster board or construction paper
- Mathew 1:21 poster

{Use the poster board to cut out huge letters spelling JESUS using the colors of the Wordless Book. J=gold; E=black; S=red; U=white; S=green. My letters were about 3 feet long. I found that I needed to support the letters, so I taped dowel rods and chopsticks to the back! Another option would be to use thin foam board posters.}

Geography: Nazareth and Bethlehem

Background: An angel appeared to Mary, explaining that she had been chosen to be the mother of the Son of God. She was to be married to Joseph, but when he was told that she was pregnant, he had a decision to make. He could marry her and accept her story; or, he could quietly put her away and not marry her.

"She will give birth to a son. You will name the son Jesus. Give him that name because he will save his people from their sins."

—Matthew 1:21 (ICB)

FUTUREFLYINGSAUCERS.COM

BIBLE LESSON AND LIFE APPLICATION

■ ■

{Ask:}

- What do you know about Joseph? [*Allow for answers. You will find that they will not know much. I had answers such as: a shepherd, Mary's husband, etc.*]

The book of Matthew tells us that Joseph was a just man. When he heard that Mary was with child and they were not married yet, Joseph knew he could legally break off their engagement. Joseph could do this publicly so everyone in town would know. He could have said loudly and clearly that the baby was not his and that he wanted nothing more to do with Mary.

However, Joseph was a just man, an honorable man. This tells us that Joseph was a man of character. He cared for Mary and wanted what was best for her. Therefore, he decided to end the engagement quietly so no one knew what really happened.

While he was thinking this over, an angel appeared to Joseph in a dream. The angel told him not to be afraid to take Mary as his wife because the baby in her was made by the Holy Spirit. The angel told him that she would have a Son. Also, he was to call the baby Jesus, because He would save His people from their sin.

Joseph awoke from his dream and did as the Lord commanded him. He took Mary to be his wife. Once the baby was born, Joseph named the baby Jesus.

Jesus is a great name. In fact, it is the name above all names. It is the name that saves people from their sins.

{Ask:}

- What is sin? [*Anything we think, say, or do that does not please God*]
- What are some examples of sin? [*Allow for answers.*]

{Hold up the J and ask:}

- What do you know about God? [*Allow for answers. Examples: holy, perfect, without sin, eternal, never changes, kind, etc.*]

Yellow helps us to remember heaven and God. God is perfect. He is holy. The Bible tells us that Jesus is God in the flesh. Therefore, Jesus is perfect and He is holy.

{Hold up the *E* and ask:}

- What do you know about people? [*Allow for answers. Examples: not perfect, selfish, temporary, etc.*]
- Can people ever do good things? [*Yes*]
- Why do people need Jesus? [*Allow for answers. Help children to see what the Scripture says in Matthew. Jesus came to save His people from their sins.*]
- Can people save themselves from their sins? [*No*]
- Can people do enough good things to show God they deserve to be saved? [*No*]

Scripture tells us that our good works are like filthy, dirty rags. We are born into sin. Because of that sin, we deserve death. HOWEVER...

{Hold up the red *S* and ask:}

- What does red remind us of? [*Blood*]

At Christmas, we set aside time to celebrate the birth of Jesus. But really, it is the death of Jesus that saves us from our sin. When we believe in our heart that Jesus is God, that He was born on this earth in flesh, and that He died and rose again, and if we confess our sin, then the blood of Jesus cleanses us from all our unrighteousness. Our dark sin does not look like that to God anymore. He sees the blood of Jesus covering us instead.

{Hold up the *U* and ask:}

- When you decide to live for Jesus, do you always obey God with what you do? [*No, we still sin.*]

Even though the blood of Jesus covers us, we still make wrong choices. Each time we ask God to forgive us, we are cleansed again of our sin. **It is a constant thing we need to do**. Whenever we recognize that we have messed up, we need to tell on ourselves to God. Jesus is the One who saves us from our sin, so we need to stay in constant contact with Him.

{Hold up the green *S*.}

Jesus was born. We are celebrating His birthday. You have a birthday every year. On each birthday you are a little bit taller, a little bit smarter, and little bit wiser. The more you learn about Jesus and spend time with Him, the more you will grow spiritually.

After Jesus saves you from sin, you need to grow. We celebrate Jesus' birthday one day a year, but we should be growing to know Jesus better every day of the year. This is how God begins to turn you into a person like Jesus. We can never be perfect like Jesus, but we can reflect Him the best we can by loving others and serving them.

What name is above all names? Jesus. The angel said Jesus will save us from our sin. He will. He will save you from your sin. Choose Jesus.

What can we learn from Joseph? We should believe what the angel told him and know that Jesus will save us from our sin.

COMMENT BOX

■ ■

THINK: What went well as you taught this lesson? What can you do better?

_____

_____

_____

_____

_____

_____

_____

_____

_____

TIP: Hang the letters in your Bible teaching area. Revisit throughout the year the meaning of the colors and why the name of Jesus is so important.

EXTRA RESOURCES

HOW TO LEAD
A CHILD TO CHRIST

■ ■

After you teach a Bible lesson, there are times when it is necessary to ask the children if they want to receive the gift of salvation through Jesus. Always have those who want to make some sort of decision leave the larger group of kids. I do this by either having them stay behind while the others leave, or taking the small group into another room. I do this because it causes the child to physically make a decision: *"Do I stay? Or not?"* This also allows for fewer distractions. (Always be sure to have another adult nearby. That's a safety rule!)

Ask many questions; you want the children to think through what they are doing. These questions should not be answered by "Yes," "No," or "Jesus." Use lots of Scripture, because you want God's Word to be working.

There is no minimum age for salvation. Even three-year-olds can recognize they are sinners and be sorry for what they do. However, you do want to be sure that the child, no matter the age, understands this lifelong commitment.

Salvation is a big deal, and you don't want a child to make a decision that is not understood or taken seriously. If at any point you sense that there is confusion or uncertainty on the child's part, say, *"I can tell that God is working in your heart. I want you to keep listening and learning."* Then dismiss that child who is not ready.

Examples of Counseling Questions:

1. Why have you decided to talk with me?

2. Why do you need Jesus as your Savior?

3. What is sin?

4. What are some examples of sin?

5. Can you do anything to get rid of sin?

6. Read Romans 3:23.

7. Who is Jesus?

8. What did Jesus do for you?

9. Read 1 Corinthians 15:3-4.

10. Read John 3:16 or Acts 16:31.

11. Would you like to pray to God and receive Jesus now?

If the child understands the questions and is answering appropriately, describe salvation as a heart change—a choice to move away from sin and toward God. If the child is serious about dealing with sin and wanting to live for Jesus, explain that he or she needs to talk to God and that talking to God is called prayer.

At this point lead the child in prayer. Have the child copy what you say or tell the child what information should be included when asking God for salvation:

- Admit to God you are a sinner.
- Say that you are sorry for those sins. Ask for forgiveness.
- Tell Jesus you believe Jesus is God's Son and that He died on the cross and rose again.
- Confess that Jesus is your Lord and Master.
- Thank God for saving you.

Once the child has prayed, read Hebrews 13:5b and 6a. Ask, *What has Jesus done for you?* This will give assurance of salvation.

Pray for that child when you are finished. Then have the child choose at least one person to tell about what happened (usually a parent).

Rejoice with the family!

It is possible you might have a situation that includes parents who are not happy about the choice made by their child. If this happens, explain the decision to the parents, but then, if at all possible, disciple that child yourself. If the child goes to another church or no church at all, check on the child when you can. Definitely pray for that young Christian.

Be sure to tell your pastor of the child's decision so he can follow up with the family and discuss baptism. If you are a parent and your child has accepted Jesus as his or her Savior, be sure to help your child grow in knowledge and service.

HOW TO BECOME AN EXCELLENT BIBLE TEACHER

▪▪▪▪▪▪▪▪▪▪▪▪▪▪▪▪▪▪▪▪▪▪▪

When teaching children, our goal is two-fold. First, we want kids to **get right** with God through a saving faith. Second, we want our children to **stay right** with God through the sanctification process.

> You, however, continue in the things you have learned and become convinced of, knowing from whom you have learned them, and that from childhood you have known the sacred writings which are able to give you the wisdom that leads to salvation through faith which is in Christ Jesus. All Scripture is inspired by God and profitable for teaching, for reproof, for correction, for training in righteousness; so that the man of God may be adequate, equipped for every good work.
>
> 2 Timothy 3:14-17 (NASB)

WHAT We Want to Teach:

We want to focus on verse 16, because if we can (1) **teach** doctrine in such a way that reveals sin, and then (2) explain how to stop sinning (**reproof**), and then (3) counsel children how to fix their sin problems (**correction**), THEN (4) they will be restored to a character of **righteousness** so God can use them for good works. This is the cycle of sanctification after salvation.

However, the cycle of sanctification does not revolve in a circle. It is more like a spiral as we grow closer to God and He works on our hearts.

We can also think of it this way: As our view of God increases, our view of ourselves decreases. (Sounds like John the Baptist!) The discrepancy is seen more and more. Jesus becomes bigger in our lives the more we know of Him. He must increase. We must decrease. Yes, we are children of God, heirs to a kingdom, but we are clothed in unrighteous rags. We need Jesus.

This is what we want for our children, whether they are our own or those we teach in the church. **We want them to view Jesus as being the One and Only Greatest Person in their lives.**

HOW We Teach This:

In order to be an excellent Bible teacher, a person must seek God first and foremost. **I fail at this.** I am not an excellent Bible teacher because of what I do, but because of what God chooses to do through me. I attempt to read the Bible every day. I attempt to make good choices. I mess up.

I think this is what makes the difference between a mediocre Bible teacher and an excellent Bible teacher: **An excellent Bible teacher daily recognizes his or her own need for a Savior**.

It is through our failings that Christ shines His light into our Bible lessons. When we explain to children how God is real, forgiving, and personal in our own lives, they will begin to search for that type of relationship as well.

How do we teach children? By allowing God to teach us. This means we need to take an honest look at ourselves, evaluate our hearts, and apply what God shows us to our teaching.

Prayerfully read through the next few questions and answer them.

Evaluation of Yourself:

1. Are you sold out to Jesus?

2. How enthusiastic are you about your teaching?

3. Are you interested in your children's lives?

4. Can you sense the needs of your children?

5. Are you a servant leader?

Evaluation of Each Bible Lesson:

1. Did you accomplish your objectives?

2. If not, why?

3.   What was weak?

4.   What was strong?

5.   What changes should you make before the next lesson or before you teach this lesson again?

Evaluation of the Teaching Year:

1.   How many salvations took place among your children?

2.   Can you see a growth of Biblical knowledge in your children?

3.   Was there growth in their spiritual heart knowledge?

"To whom would He teach knowledge,
And to whom would He interpret the message?
Those just weaned from milk?
Those just taken from the breast?
"For He says,
'Order on order, order on order,
Line on line, line on line,
A little here, a little there.'"

Isaiah 28:9-10 (NASB)

Biblical knowledge, or learning the Scriptures, takes a life time. It involves a little truth here and a little lesson there, step by step. We Bible teachers want our children to discover for themselves what they *ought* to do, so that through loving God, they will *obey* Him regardless of any obstacles. **A committed will to obey God equals a changed life.**

A NOTE FROM THE AUTHOR

■ ■ ■ ■ ■ ■ ■ ■ ■ ■ ■ ■ ■ ■ ■ ■ ■ ■ ■

Friend, I encourage you. You hold the living, powerful Word of God in your hands. Use it wisely. Read it lovingly. Teach from it enthusiastically. Love powerfully. **Be Excellent!**

Your Servant,

Anne Marie

FutureFlyingSaucers.com

COLORING PAGES

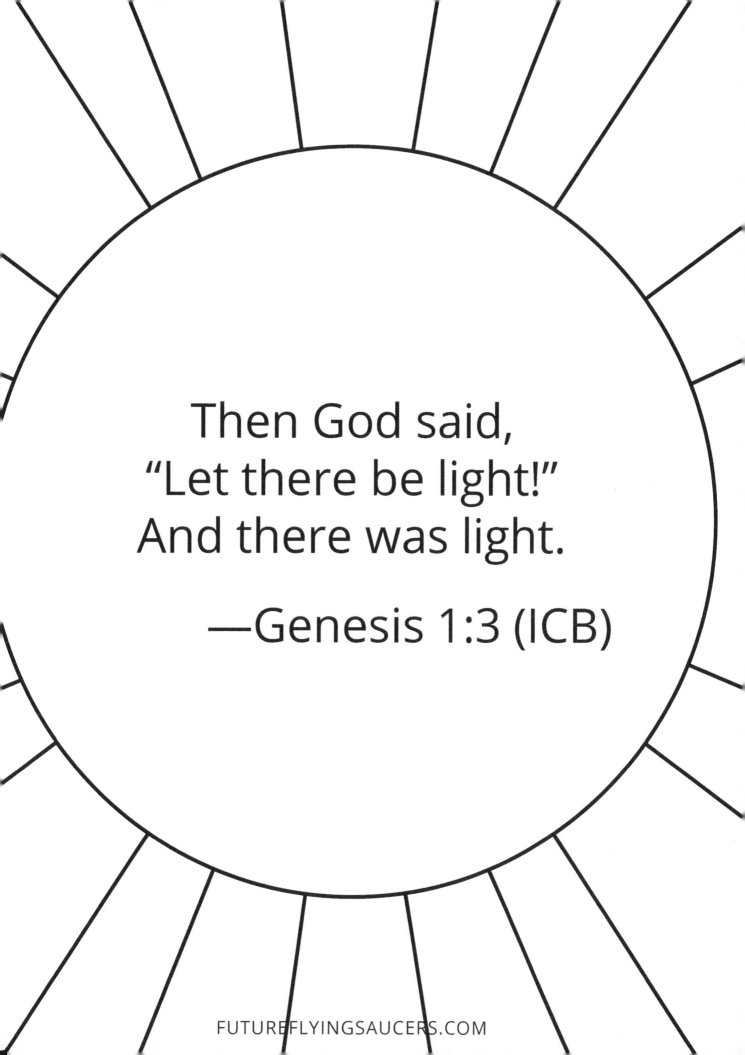

Then God said,
"Let there be light!"
And there was light.

—Genesis 1:3 (ICB)

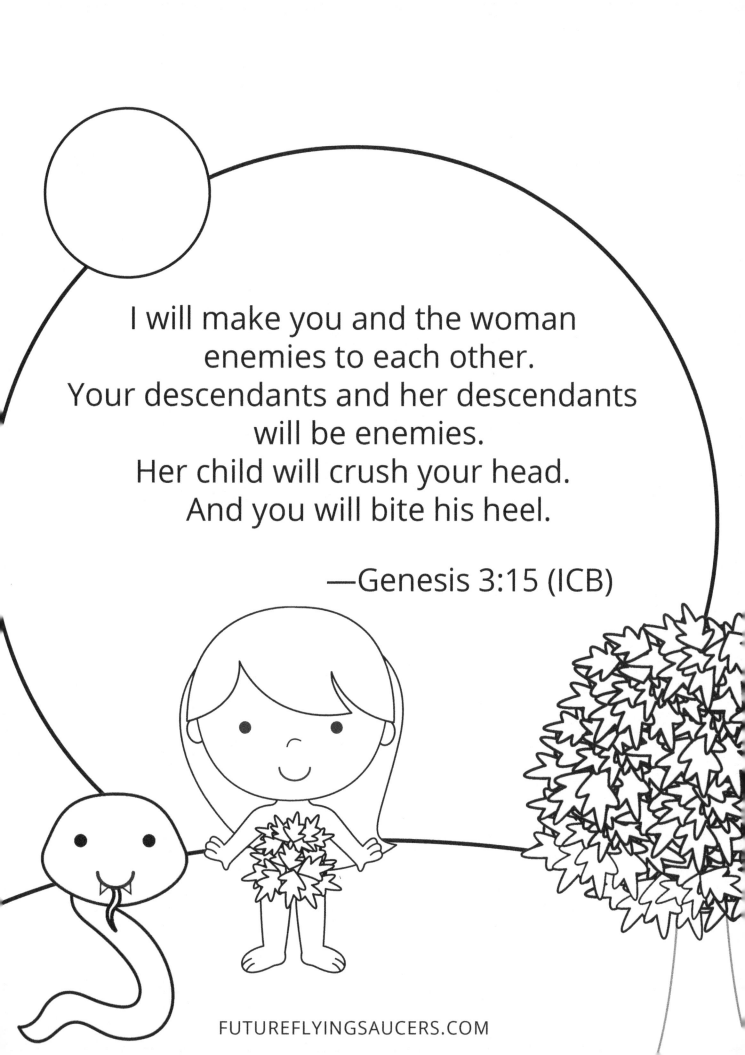

I will make you and the woman
enemies to each other.
Your descendants and her descendants
will be enemies.
Her child will crush your head.
And you will bite his heel.

—Genesis 3:15 (ICB)

"If you do good, I will accept you.
But if you do not do good,
sin is ready to attack you.
Sin wants you.
But you must rule over it."

—Genesis 4:7 (ICB)

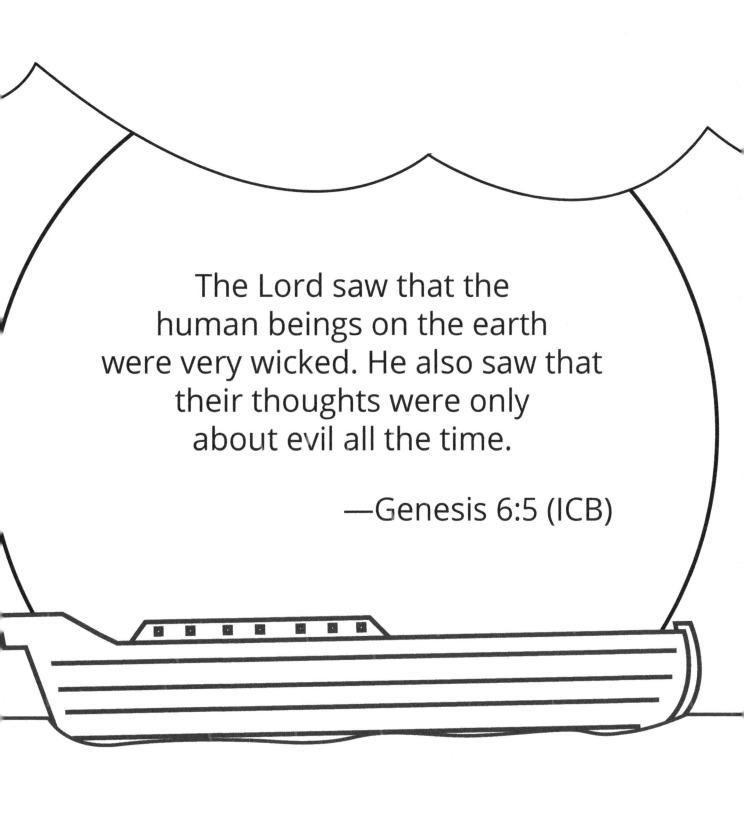

The Lord saw that the
human beings on the earth
were very wicked. He also saw that
their thoughts were only
about evil all the time.

—Genesis 6:5 (ICB)

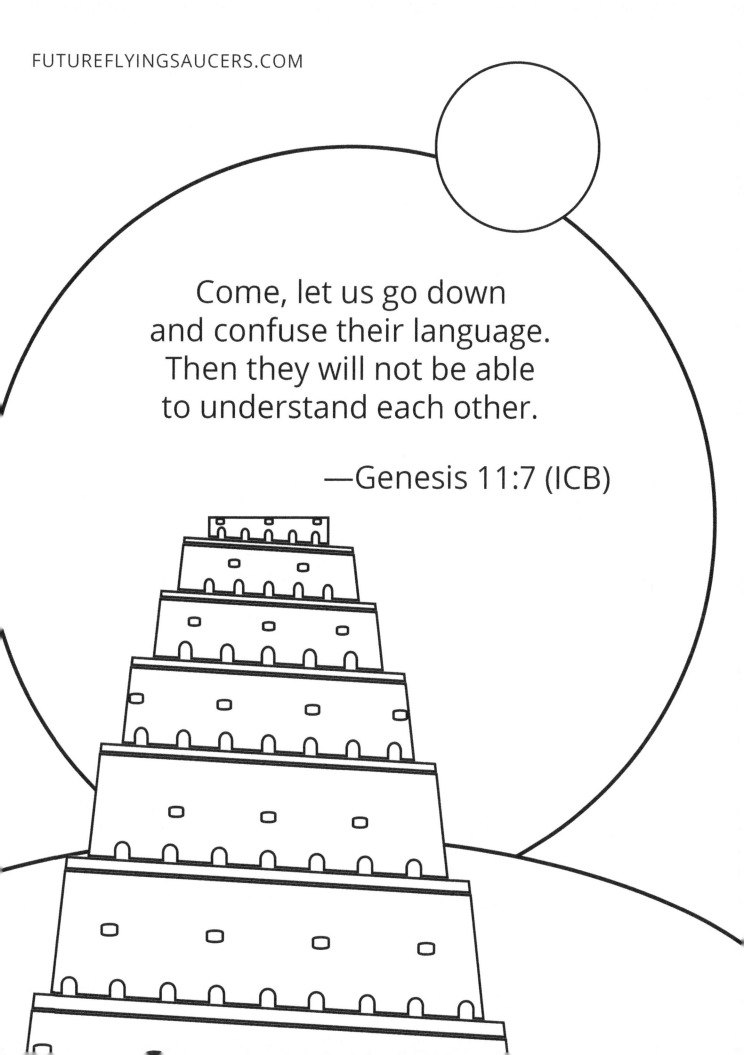

Come, let us go down
and confuse their language.
Then they will not be able
to understand each other.

—Genesis 11:7 (ICB)

Then the Lord said to Abram,
"Leave your country, your relatives
and your father's family.
Go to the land I will show you."

—Genesis 12:1 (ICB)

So Abraham went and
took the sheep and killed it.
He offered it as a whole
burnt offering to God.
Abraham's son was saved.

—Genesis 22:13b (ICB)

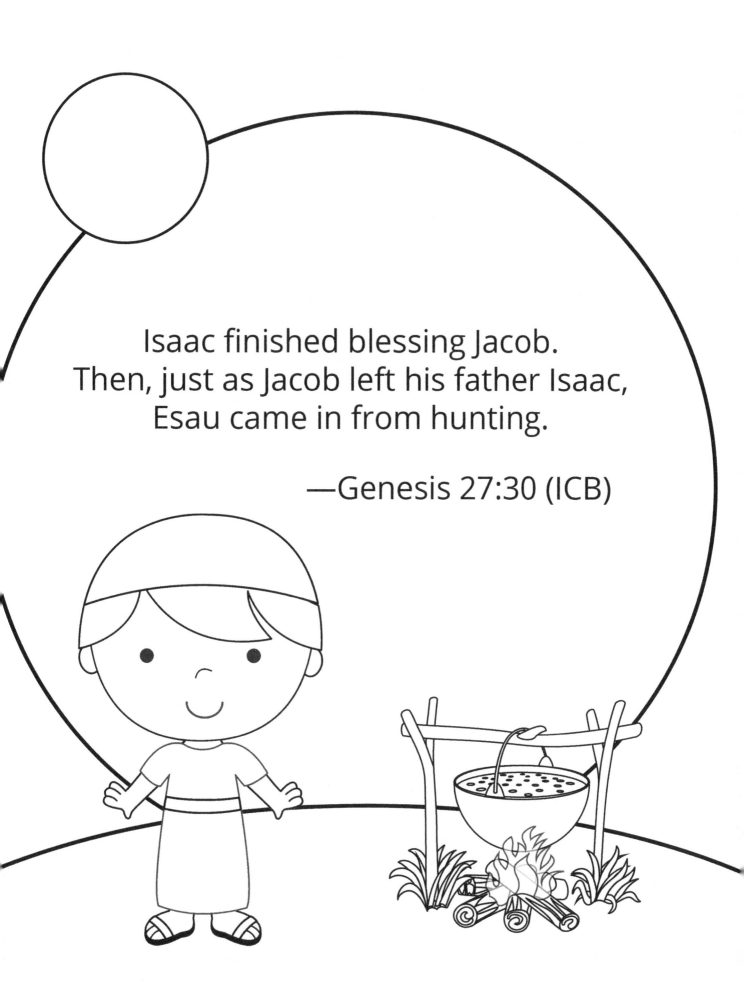

Isaac finished blessing Jacob.
Then, just as Jacob left his father Isaac,
Esau came in from hunting.

—Genesis 27:30 (ICB)

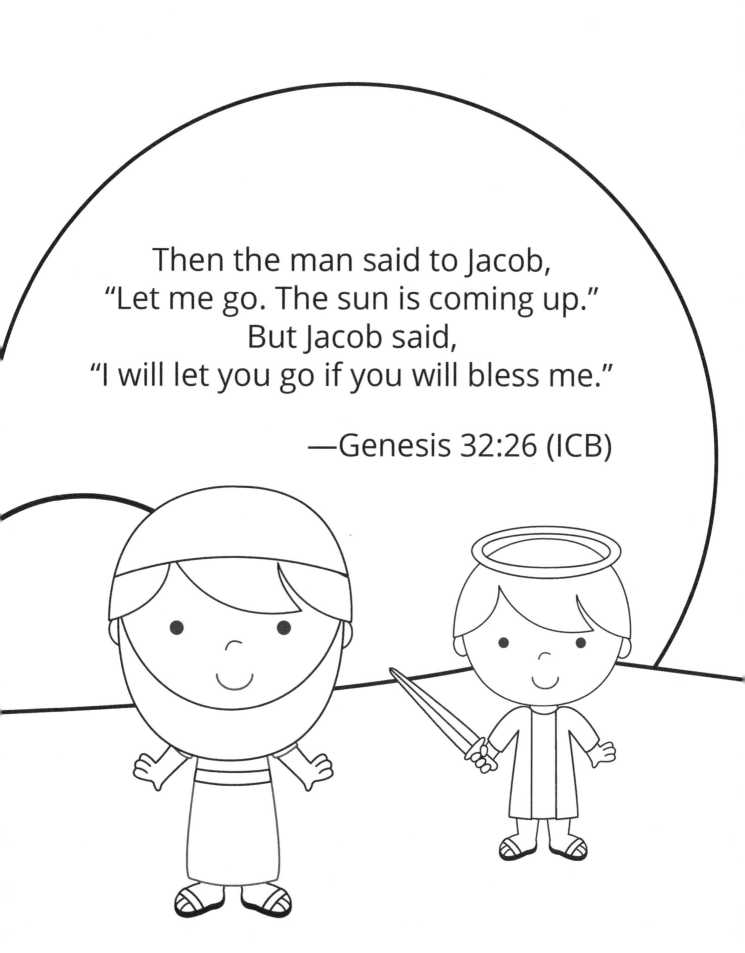

Then the man said to Jacob,
"Let me go. The sun is coming up."
But Jacob said,
"I will let you go if you will bless me."

—Genesis 32:26 (ICB)

So God sent me here ahead of you. This was to make sure you have some descendants left on earth. And it was to keep you alive in an amazing way.

—Genesis 45:7 (ICB)

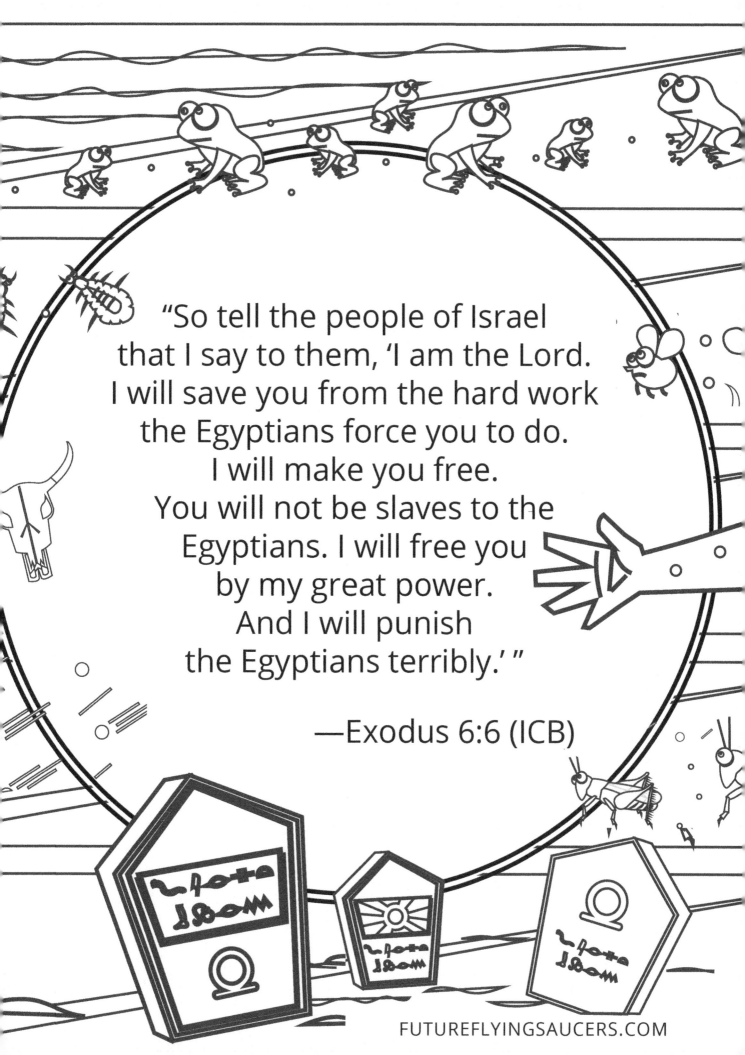

"So tell the people of Israel
that I say to them, 'I am the Lord.
I will save you from the hard work
the Egyptians force you to do.
I will make you free.
You will not be slaves to the
Egyptians. I will free you
by my great power.
And I will punish
the Egyptians terribly.'"

—Exodus 6:6 (ICB)

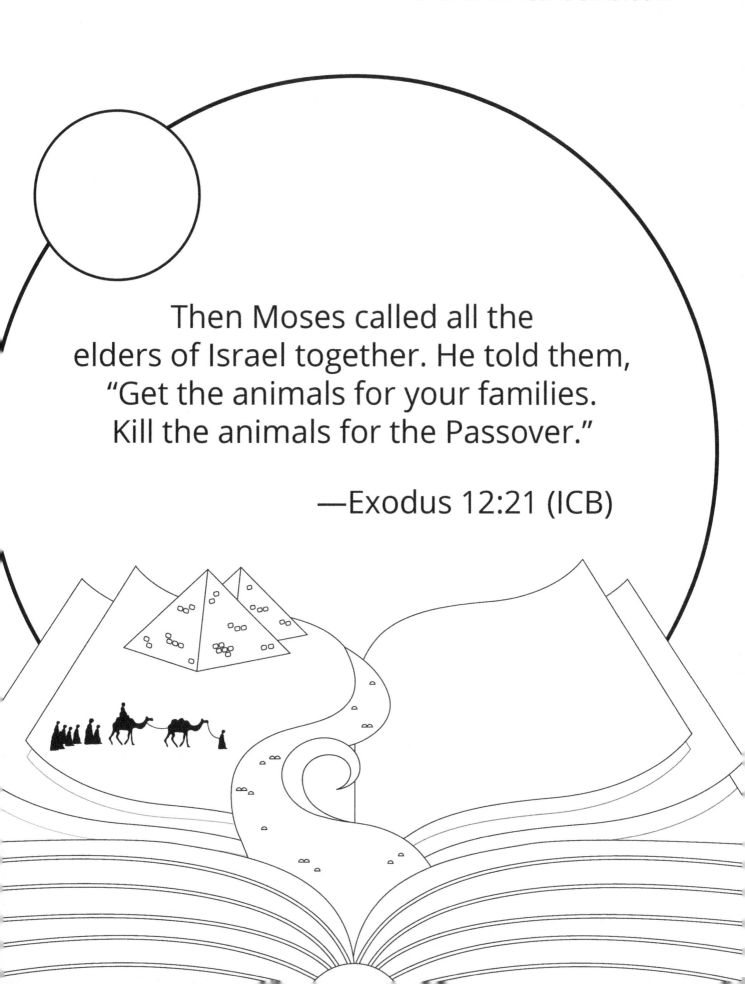

Then Moses called all the
elders of Israel together. He told them,
"Get the animals for your families.
Kill the animals for the Passover."

—Exodus 12:21 (ICB)

"I am the Lord your God.
I brought you out of the
land of Egypt where
you were slaves.
You must not have any
other gods except me."

—Exodus 20:2-3 (ICB)

Then Caleb told the people
near Moses to be quiet.
Caleb said, "We should go up and
take the land for ourselves.
We can do it."

—Numbers 13:30 (ICB)

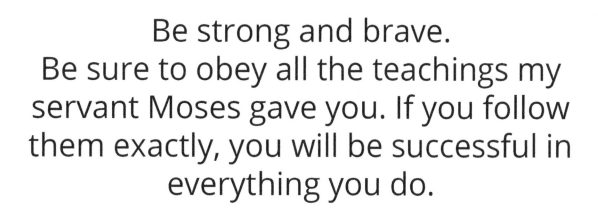

Be strong and brave.
Be sure to obey all the teachings my servant Moses gave you. If you follow them exactly, you will be successful in everything you do.

—Joshua 1:7 (ICB)

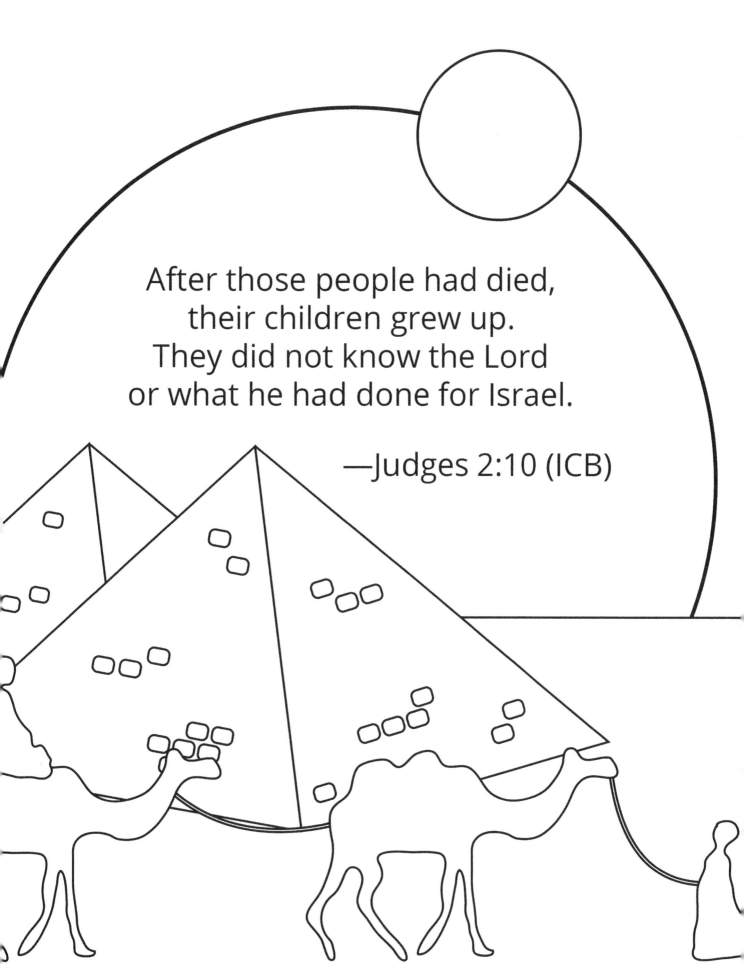

After those people had died,
their children grew up.
They did not know the Lord
or what he had done for Israel.

—Judges 2:10 (ICB)

The Lord came and stood there. He called as he had before. He said, "Samuel, Samuel!" Samuel said, "Speak, Lord. I am your servant, and I am listening."

—1 Samuel 3:10 (ICB)

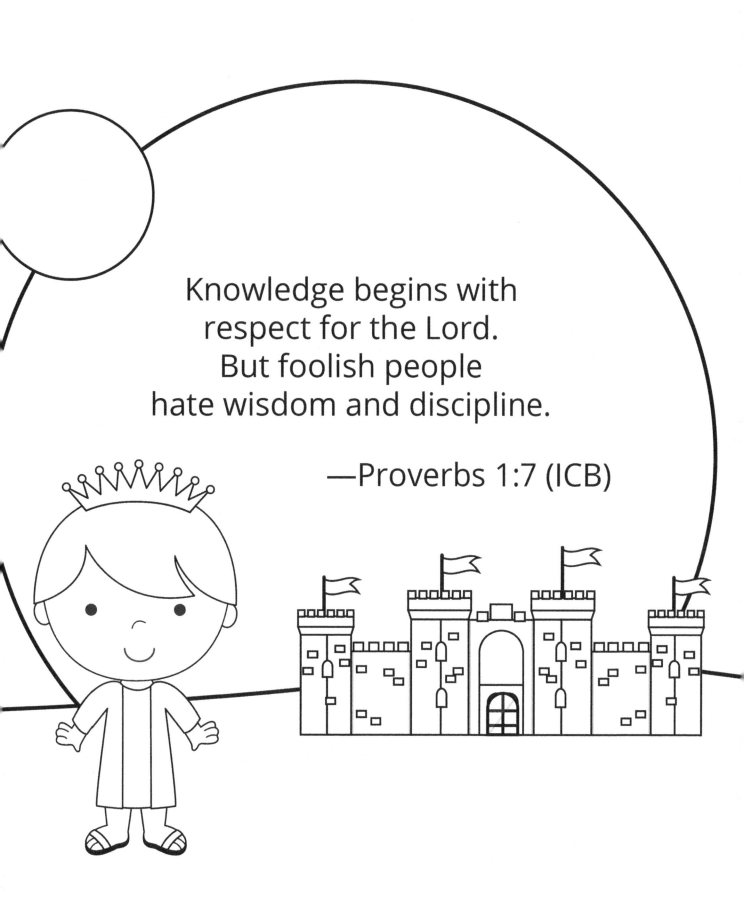

Knowledge begins with
respect for the Lord.
But foolish people
hate wisdom and discipline.

—Proverbs 1:7 (ICB)

So the king did not do
what the people wanted.
The Lord caused this to happen.

—1 Kings 12:15a (ICB)

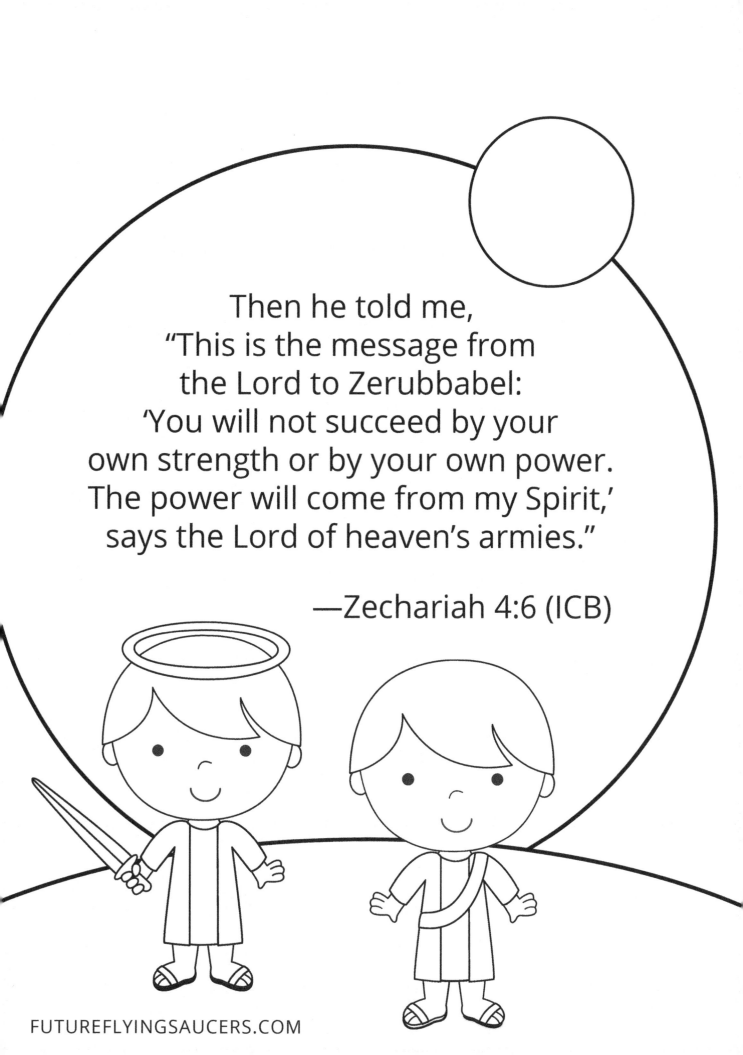

Then he told me,
"This is the message from
the Lord to Zerubbabel:
'You will not succeed by your
own strength or by your own power.
The power will come from my Spirit,'
says the Lord of heaven's armies."

—Zechariah 4:6 (ICB)

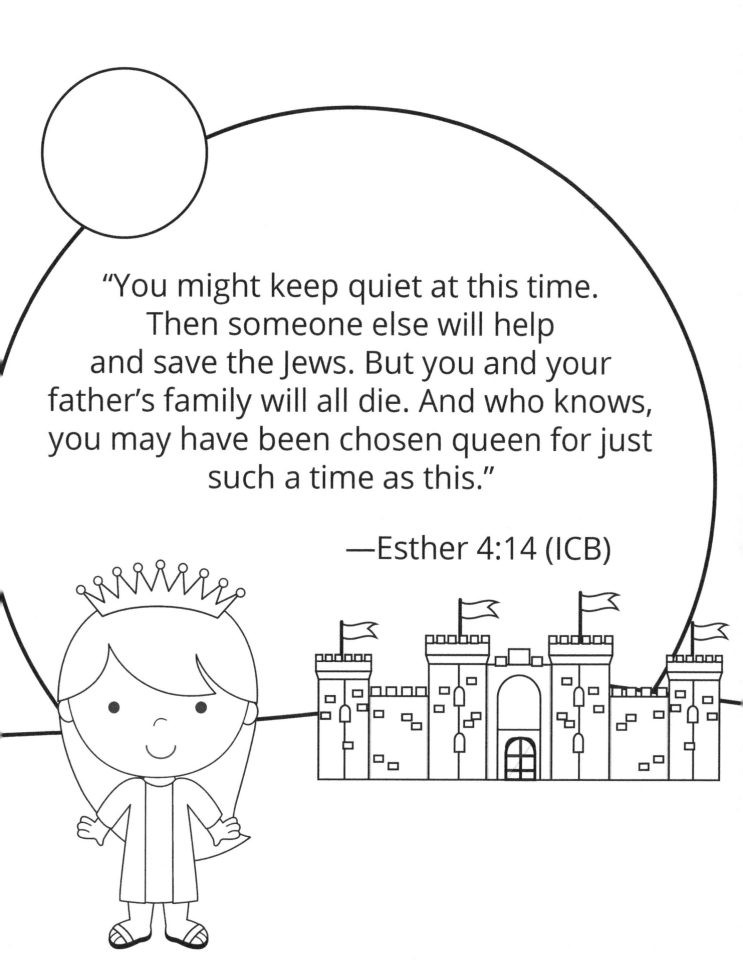

"You might keep quiet at this time.
Then someone else will help
and save the Jews. But you and your
father's family will all die. And who knows,
you may have been chosen queen for just
such a time as this."

—Esther 4:14 (ICB)

"But now, our God,
what can we say after you
have done all this?
We have disobeyed
your commands."

—Ezra 9:10 (ICB)

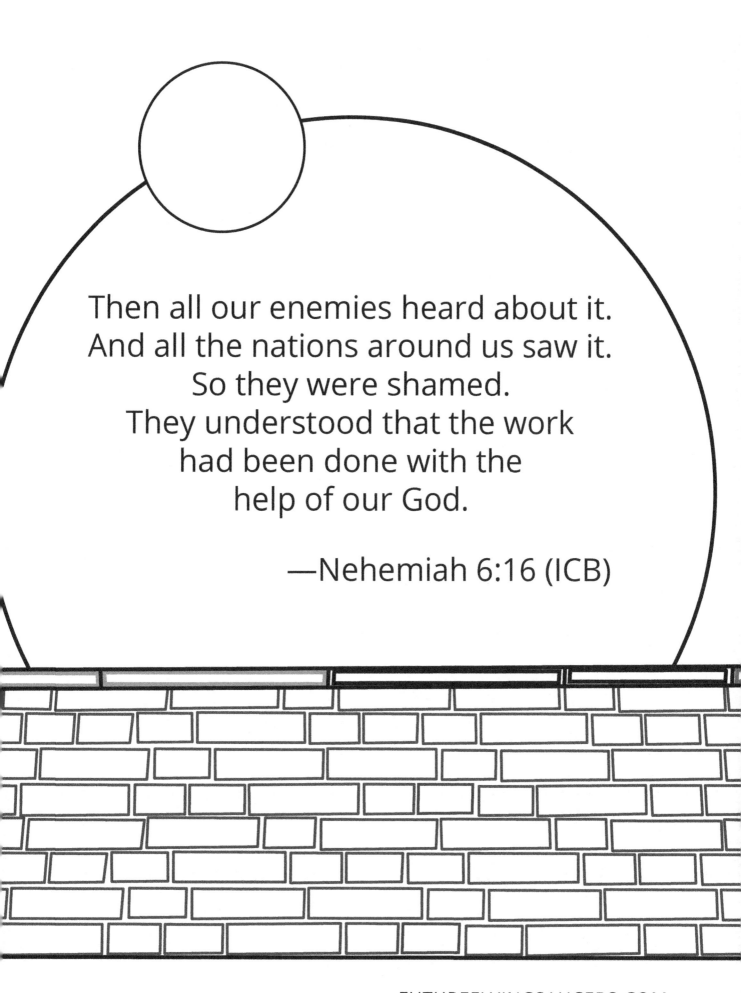

Then all our enemies heard about it.
And all the nations around us saw it.
So they were shamed.
They understood that the work
had been done with the
help of our God.

—Nehemiah 6:16 (ICB)

But when the right time came,
God sent his Son. His Son was born of a
woman and lived under the law.

—Galatians 4:4 (ICB)

"She will give birth to a son.
You will name the son Jesus.
Give him that name because he will save
his people from their sins."

—Matthew 1:21 (ICB)

For more ideas, lessons, coloring pages, games, etc., go to my Pinterest boards. I've found all kinds of fun stuff for you!

Be sure to leave a **5 star review** on the website (Amazon, etc.) where you purchased this book.

Made in the USA
Coppell, TX
15 September 2020